The Multi-Age Learning Community in Action

The Multi-Age Learning Community in Action

Creating a Caring School Environment for All Children

Barbara Cozza

ROWMAN & LITTLEFIELD
Lanham • Boulder • New York • London

Published by Rowman & Littlefield
A wholly owned subsidiary of The Rowman & Littlefield Publishing Group, Inc.
4501 Forbes Boulevard, Suite 200, Lanham, Maryland 20706
www.rowman.com

Unit A, Whitacre Mews, 26-34 Stannary Street, London SE11 4AB

British Library Cataloguing in Publication Information Available

Library of Congress Cataloging-in-Publication Data

Names: Cozza, Barbara, author.
Title: The multiage learning community in action : creating a caring school
   environment for all children / Barbara Cozza.
Description: Lanham, Maryland : Rowman & Littlefield, 2017. | Includes
   bibliographical references.
Identifiers: LCCN 2017025842 (print) | LCCN 2017040628 (ebook) | ISBN
   9781475837759 (electronic) | ISBN 9781475837735 (hardback : alk. paper) |
   ISBN 9781475837742 (pbk. : alk. paper)
Subjects: LCSH: Nongraded schools. | Individualized instruction. | Active
   learning. | Teaching teams. | School environment.
Classification: LCC LB1029.N6 (ebook) | LCC LB1029.N6 C695 2017 (print) | DDC
   371.3—dc23
LC record available at https://lccn.loc.gov/2017025842

Printed in the United States of America

To Sophie and Max Cozza.
These very young children represent our future leaders.

It is my intent that we encourage educators to re-culture our schools so that *all* children benefit from caring school environments that target the individual needs of the learners in effective ways. All children should have the opportunity to become the very best they can be.

Contents

Part IV: Assessments and Systemic Change

Appendixes

Foreword

I began teaching quite a while ago. I was young and inexperienced in most things when I was hired to teach reading and language arts to seventh graders in what was then a rural junior high school. I was lacking in many ways. I had not been an education major in college, had never taken a course in teaching reading, and had not previously taught adolescents. The school, too, had its gaps. It was woefully short of supplies like paper, art materials, books for kids to read in a reading class, and even student desks. There was no professional development program. I didn't know there might have been. My intent was to stay in that school for a year or two and then move on to a school in the city where I lived at the time. Yet I stayed in that school for 20 years and developed a passion for teaching that has never waned. It was a petri dish for enthusiastic and empowered teachers.

Certainly a primary reason for my love affair with the school and my role in it was the students I taught. They were a varied bunch in terms of background, entry points, and comfort with formal schooling, but they were also teetering between childhood and adulthood in ways that brought forth great silliness and astonishing insight at unpredictable intervals. They were more wide-eyed than skeptical, and daily, they were my teachers about life. Middle school was, and still is, my briar patch.

The other reason I found the work I did to be so deeply satisfying, however, was the environment in which my colleagues and I taught. Lacking most of the material supports teachers to turn to as they plan their teaching, my teaching partners and I turned to one another. We were given the freedom to be generative and encouraged to learn from one another. Over the years, a core group of us who taught the same subject formally met together weekly to share ideas, troubleshoot, and plan. Informally, we were together more often than that—in hallways between classes, in one another's rooms at the end of the day, on the phone in the evening.

We decided together what our students needed to learn the fundamental skills of reading, writing, oral communication, media literacy, literature, and so on. We looked for contexts in which we could teach those skills with the idea that the contexts issued the invitations to learn and the skills were embedded into those contexts in ways that made the skills themselves seem important rather than rote or imposed. We struggled at length for effective ways to help our large population of very weak readers make up for lost time, how to help our large population of very strong readers continue to stretch, and how to do both those things in a classroom that belonged equally to every learner.

We hunted for instructional strategies that would let us reach out to students differently, based on their varied strengths, needs, and interests. We invented a good number of strategies ourselves. We grappled with schedules and divisions of time within schedules and ways to work with the class as a whole while ensuring enough time to meet our students where they were individually.

We created common lesson plans with the understanding that each of us could bring our own talents and personalities to bear on those plans in ways we determined would be of greatest value to our own students. We devised routines that addressed both group and individual needs, and guidelines for working with our students to be sure the routines were effective in supporting student success. We developed criteria for success, record-keeping mechanisms that allowed us to know how students were progressing toward those goals—even though they often worked on tasks that were not a match for everyone else's tasks. Ultimately, we even created a grading system that reflected our aspirations for both individuals and the group.

We developed our own pre-assessments—somewhat primitive by current measure, but quite useful nonetheless. We gathered and analyzed standardized test data at the end of each year to help us look back and ahead. We even worked with the state's department of education and a nearby university to do formal studies of our students' growth. And we kept at all of that for nearly two decades.

Here's what resulted from that work. Our students, who typically demonstrated at least an eight-year span of readiness, grew academically far more than their peers in other classrooms, and they consistently rated this class as their favorite. Beyond that, their teachers grew remarkably as professional thinkers and problem solvers. We saw teaching as a highly creative profession. It extended our capacity beyond any scope we'd have imagined.

I'd confidently wager that we developed a depth and breadth of pedagogical understanding that would far exceed what we'd have achieved through typical professional development experiences. We owned what we did in our classrooms—successful and abysmal—because together, we crafted, studied, tested, revised them, and began the cycle again—and again. Nothing was dictated or packaged. We became our students' best advocates—and our own.

I'm a fan of multi-age classrooms taught as they are described in this book. In truth, I think all classrooms are multi-age in a very real sense. This book describes with care and detail how to think about and plan for teaching children who would typically be divided into two separate grades, and who are intentionally placed together with the goal of enabling them to grow from their entry points with curriculum and instruction that meets them where they are and moves them forward. That seems to me to be a decision rooted in the reality of the variability of learners of any given age.

Beyond the practicality of multi-age configurations, however, as I read the book, I was reminded of the professional and personal richness I experienced through the years when working with my colleagues in the school that "grew us all up" as teachers. To be sure, we had our share of days that were more about despair than victory, working often with a sense of being lost in a swamp. Nonetheless, our mission was to create the most defensible and engaging method we could muster to support the success of our remarkably diverse learners and we were able to think comprehensively, fluidly, and collegially in a way that taught us to deal with the complexity of each element of teaching and learning, and with the interdependence among them. In that process, we became architects of curriculum, instructional inventors, assessment and grading pioneers, shapers of schedules, and partners with our students.

This book offers a sound blueprint for proactive and effective teaching of students who differ in their entry points into learning. In addition, it provides guidance for the kind of thinking, planning, and reflection that creates teachers who know their craft deeply and own its outcomes. I am hopeful that it opens the way to this sort of professionalism and leadership for many student-focused teachers.

Carol Ann Tomlinson, Ed.D.
William Clay Parrish Jr. Professor and Chair,
Educational Leadership, Foundations, and Policy,
Curry School of Education, University of Virginia

Preface

Why Multi-Age Our School Classrooms?

At a small elementary school in a northeastern town in the United States the staff remains baffled. Even though the principal and teachers work diligently at integrating Common Core State Standards, results on the high stakes tests continue to decline. The teachers and school leaders feel they are doing all they can do based on their current knowledgebase and skills. They teach from textbooks, they connect to Smart Board tasks, and they give different worksheets to students to differentiate lessons for students. They even allow low-performing students to read from the classroom Chromebooks.

The school district staff members are concerned about how to improve performance of students in this school. The district has purchased a variety of curriculum guides, teaching programs, and testing systems. The school leader and district team discuss the needs of the school program by conducting ongoing conversations on how to improve the teaching and learning processes in this school—and student scores are still not where they should be.

As I move through many school buildings, this school scenario occurs regularly across the nation. In many districts and schools, the teaching and learning process is a jumble of initiatives that are created by educators that have good intentions. School leaders and teachers purchase materials, convene meetings, and create curriculum plans with little attention to how these elements connect as a whole for learners' needs. Most educators do not integrate a vision plan that can turn their concepts of schooling into reality.

They do not ground their ideas with research and best practices (Carr & Harris, 2001). I believe that the answer for improving student performance is to focus on the learner and then build the school community around the student's needs.

This book is about rethinking how schools should build a learning community that connects to what each learner needs to excel in school for the 21st century. I suspect that many educators want the very best learning environment for their students. For this reason, we see pockets of schools integrating teacher teams that look at data. We view professional learning communities scheduling curriculum planning meetings. We observe how teachers and administrators attempt to share leadership ideas to encourage the effective implementation of instruction.

What we see is that these educators go through the motions for making change in schools. I am sure these educators' hearts are in the right place. However, the real issue is not addressed. Our schools do not put the learner first and then build what the learner needs. Teachers tend to control students' learning considering what the curriculum tells them. Teachers present concepts to learners based on what teachers think students need. What we find is that specific assignments do not allow for different levels of abilities. One curriculum does not fit all.

Teachers hesitate to allow students to work collaboratively with other students because the noise level is loud. Too often the curriculum is a collection of scripts from textbook companies. This approach does not allow for independent thinking and learning for the student and the teacher. As educators, we need to stop imposing what we think students should do in a lesson. We need to present concepts and see how students are able to make sense of the information.

This multi-age school program puts the learner first. This multi-age program encourages a reform in education that concentrates on achievement that best meets the needs of the learner without disrupting the mandates of the curricula. It is an agenda that targets one's own prior experiences, background knowledge, and cognitive capabilities. The reason for multi-age classrooms is to meet a student's individual or personalized learning needs because all students are at different levels of learning. Differentiation processes are embedded in the everyday events of the teaching and learning processes because the curriculum is adapted for each learner.

This multi-age school reform project begins by building caring school environments that target students' needs and encourage relational trust among teachers, parents, and school leaders. These caring and trusting elements in schools are found in how reliable the groups and individuals perform in a collective manner (Tarter, Bliss, & Hoy, 1989).

There are six components of trust that are integrated (Hoy & Tschannen-Moran, 1999): all school members are caring and nurturing to all; groups get along and show good will toward others; everyone is counted on to do what they say they will do; all school members accept responsibility for one's actions; and, all members freely share information and always try to be transparent with school information.

The school reform political climate today focuses on *schools of choice* and school environments that focus on the *personalized learning needs* of all learners. This book accomplishes both agendas.

This book discusses how to transform schools using a multi-age framework labeled the Multi-Age Learning Community (MAC). It suggests a professional development plan and discusses effective strategies to help schools get started. It is important that schools realize that these program components do not need to be implemented all at once.

It is not imperative for all of these program components to be adopted on the onset; rather they may be layered as the program develops. Any rural, suburban, urban, or international school can take on elements of the program based on the needs of the school system. These schools can be generated from public, private, or other international agendas.

The MAC program is different from other nongraded school agendas. This program integrates multi-age students and integrates quality strategies for effective teaching and learning for the 21st century.

MULTI-AGE DEFINED

The overarching goal of a multi-age learning environment is to target individual needs, develop problem solvers, communicators, and high-level thinkers. These qualities prepare our students for college and career readiness that our Common Core State Standards document emphasizes, and these characteristics allow students to be prepared for society's needs in the 21st century. Please realize that this program can adjust to any curriculum reform movement that changes the state standards.

The sign of the times in education tells us that we as educators need to educate all students with a rigorous program that encourages deep understanding. The Common Core State Standards Initiative (2010) are emphasizing this type of perspective. If you look closely at the standards, it becomes quite evident that grade levels are similar and that teachers should cross-grade standards to meet the needs of each individual student. Hence, in a multi-age classroom, planning for this connection happens in a natural manner.

I have a preliminary theory about why this school reform project is important to our school systems. This program assists with trying to answer the increasing pressure of all school systems to produce better results than they have ever produced. The real challenge is to ask all schools to educate all students to high levels of learning with rigorous strategies. The problem is that schools do not know how to apply this idea in every classroom for every student.

INTERNATIONAL COMMUNITIES

Why are schools under such pressure? Based on international assessments, our nation's schools do not perform as well as many of the global communities. As an outcome, many job opportunities in our country are given to much more capable mathematicians, scientists, and engineers from other countries. In the United States, we do have more diversity in student population and achievement than our international peers.

Clearly we must make needed changes in order to educate all students to high levels and prepare them for the 21st-century skills of information technology, problem solving, collaboration, and higher-level thinking.

It is appropriate to consider Finland's school organization and processes. Finland follows the idea that children should learn in a "minimally invasive education environment" which relates to the idea that children can learn a significant amount of knowledge and understanding in an unsupervised environment by themselves, interacting with other students and by helping one another.

One other important point to make is that the Finnish schools take on a more developmental approach to learning based on where each student is and adjusting curricula to fit the student and then continue to build on the knowledge of the learner based on the learner's needs (Sahlberg, 2015). These ideas connect to the established philosophy of the multi-age learning environment on some levels.

MAC as an Organizational Process

The pressure to increase student performance has caused schools to consider a schoolwide framework that concentrates on important elements: effective organization, planning, collaboration, and assessment. However, how the process in which this type of schooling should be carried out is still somewhat vague to them.

It is typical that we find principals, coaches, and staff developers entering classrooms, from time to time, observing and conversing with teachers on the best solutions for implementing effective strategies. The problem is that common language does not exist between these educators. They all have their own perspectives of what effective strategies should be for producing an increase in student achievement. For a school to be successful, all school community members should participate in making critical decisions about how to change the school system.

A school environment has an internal structure and norms that support effective teaching and learning practices. Through a multi-age organization, these educators are given the appropriate knowledgebase to succeed. The administration, teachers, coaches, staff developers, and sometimes parents have numerous conversations in and out of the classroom to discuss the appropriate processes that meet the vision of the multi-age classroom organization. Teachers are not told what to do, they are asked to reflect on practices and take the next steps for initiating effective strategies for improving student learning.

The MAC process is about modeling, sharing ideas, observing, and understanding how to solve problems to ensure teacher and student learning. Debriefing about successes and areas that need improvement are regular events. What is encouraged is that these educators in the school environment learn to take control of their own practices to move to a more sustained improvement process by continuing to take the next step forward.

MAC as a Culture-Building Process

The school culture is very different for a MAC environment. Teachers and administrators no longer work in isolation. Rather, all school staff work together, share ideas and resources, plan together, lead and support others to the next step of the learning process, and have ongoing conversations. These educators discuss the best practice for moving ahead with the school vision action plan and objectives. Professional development is embedded into the everyday activities of the school.

The debriefing sessions between the educational leader, teacher leader, school's coach, and professional development staff give direction to what curriculum to teach, how to implement lessons, how to assess students, and how to keep students engaged in the learning process.

Administrators are asked to take on the role of curriculum leader assisting with identifying vision and objectives, aligning curriculum with Common Core State Standards across grade levels, maintaining a collaborative culture, and facilitating meaningful change (DuFour & Marzano, 2011). Teacher leaders begin to design curriculum around specific topics that include multi-age teaching and learning and interdisciplinary studies.

Instructional rounds are integrated into the program with a focus on two primary learning goals (City, Elmore, Fiarman, & Teitel, 2010): build skills of teachers by coming to a common understanding of effective practice, and support instructional improvement. The lesson study research group (Lewis & Hurd, 2011; Lewis, Perry, & Murata, 2006; Takahaski, Wantanabe, Yoshida, & Wang-Iverson 2005; Watanabe, Takahashi, & Yoshida, 2008) works to improve lesson implementation. MAC lesson study teams create a model lesson and then observe a teacher implementing it. The teams focus on what students are doing, keep thorough observation field notes, and debrief with discussion and debate over lesson issues.

This type of learning environment becomes a family of a *community of learners* that have one mission in mind—to educate each student with rigorous learning to succeed in the 21st century.

MAC as a Learning Process

The learning process for improving student performance does not happen automatically. Administrators and teachers do not have all the best answers to make success happen in the classrooms. The best solution for school improvement is to gain necessary information about student performance through multiple data sources, analyze the data, and then use effective instructional practices to improve the teaching and learning processes. Hence, the multi-age learning environment embeds a process of teaching and learning that has an internal structure to offer quality instruction to all students.

In a multi-age environment, each student is learning through student-to-student interaction, teacher or student modeling, and fluid grouping situations to target individual or personal needs, independent learning through self-directed projects, group problem-solving work, inquiry investigations, learning centers, and communicating to others about topics across the curriculum. It is important to note that the multi-age learning environment is not just embedding differentiated instructional practices (that is required in all classrooms today) but, this setting depends on a fluid grouping model.

Norms for this learning setting allow for teachers and students to share ideas, learn from each other, appreciate differences, gain an understanding of different perspectives, and learn to get along and take on leadership roles. Students are members of a *community of learners*. In this type of community setting, students do not always find answers, but they explore, investigate, and reflect on ideas to generate the best and reasonable solutions. They learn to respect a variety of ideas and they debrief and reflect on what they have learned and what they still have questions about.

A BRIEF OVERVIEW OF THE BOOK

This book is intended to assist educators at all levels of all school organizations, as well as give policymakers quality information on how to transform schools into multi-age classrooms. This book is divided into four parts that explain both the theory and the practice of effective strategies for the multi-age school program: Organizational Practice, Building Culture, Learning Processes, and Assessment and Systemic Improvement.

There are specific basic principles and practices that are integrated into a quality and effective framework discussed in the chapters of this book. Each chapter begins with a vignette based on my experiences in multi-age schools and concludes with an educator's reflection to recap the concepts in the chapter.

Each chapter also integrates *snapshots* that are short real-to-life passages that bring to life concepts discussed in the chapter. Although this book discusses multi-age schools, these ideas may be applied to all school environments. To accommodate all school programs, at the end of each chapter, a section titled "Application for All Schools" is a framework that discusses just how to apply chapter concepts in any school or classroom program. It is recommended that the reader review the book one time in sequence and then reread each chapter as needed, to give meaning to the reader's purpose. All names in the book are pseudonyms.

Part I: Organizational Practice

The organizational practices are described in chapter 1 and chapter 2. The chapters include elements that form a foundation from which participants build their understanding of the program framework over time.

Chapter 1 includes how a school organization creates vision and why a school theme provides a framework for a coherent teaching and learning setting. The professional learning community model is emphasized and integrated into the framework of how administrators and teachers engage in the practice of MAC. Instructional rounds and lesson study sessions are defined.

Chapter 2 defines the administrator's role as shared leader, instructional planner, and supporter. The teacher's role is defined as collaborator. The teacher leader's role integrates curriculum mapping, teaming with others, supporting lessons, and reflecting on practices.

Part II: Culture Building

The culture-building process, discussed in chapters 3 and 4, is very important to this program because it emphasizes collaboration agendas. It points out that schools are no longer environments where teachers and learners work in isolation. In chapters 3 and 4, there is discussion on how to build caring environments that integrate relational trust components that connect to effective education communities.

Chapter 3 describes case studies of school environments. This chapter defines the term "community of learners" and discusses how to prepare educators, parents, and students in forming such a community. Chapter 3 includes ways that a collaborative community is formed and what strategies may be used to assist with the collaboration in a school district and school building. Elements for a caring and trusting environment are defined with real-to-life examples.

Chapter 4 answers many of the questions that arise when educators are forming this new school culture. These questions include: Who should be involved? How large should collaborative teams be? What kinds of resources, including time, are needed? What kinds of commitments and understandings should the MAC group have? How does one get buy-in from administrators, teachers, and parents? What should be done from the beginning during phase 1 of the program? What can the project define over time through phase 2 and 3?

Part III: The Learning Process

The learning process, discussed in chapters 5–7, integrates all curriculum ideas and instructional strategies that should be considered for implementation in this multi-age program.

Chapter 5 defines the appropriate instructional components for implementing a multi-age classroom: direct instruction (workshop style), defining learning expectations short- and long-term, differentiated teaching and learning, collaborative grouping, fluid grouping, scaffolding, independent learning, project-based instruction, individualized instruction, and learning centers. This chapter also describes what a physical learning environment looks like to meet the needs of this multi-age program. The chapter describes what a teacher should know and do when managing a multi-age classroom.

Chapter 6 outlines how to curriculum plan for different ages in all subject areas. Some questions that are considered: How are different subjects taught to a diverse group of learners? What are Reading Workshop, Math Workshop, and Writing Workshop in a multi-age setting?

Chapter 7 discusses how to connect multi-age learning in science and social studies. An interdisciplinary approach is emphasized. Curriculum cycles are defined a framework that eliminates having some students repeat the same topics of study each year. Brain research ideas connect to interdisciplinary teaching and learning strategies. There is a focus on project-based learning, independent learning, orbital studies, and differentiation for all learners that include English Language Learners and Special Needs students.

Part IV: Assessments and Systemic Change

Assessment and systemic change, outlined in chapters 8 and 9, allows for educators to reflect on the program to understand successes and improvement areas based on short- and long-term goals. Chapter 10 includes a plan for evaluating a school program.

Chapter 8 discusses and presents examples of ongoing formative assessment strategies that are used in all multi-age classrooms and for all subject areas. It also presents ideas on how a student portfolio system is constructed and implemented.

Chapter 9 shows what happens beyond the program using evidence from practice. The term "problem of practice" is defined using examples from professional learning communities, classroom instructional rounds, and lesson study sessions.

Chapter 10 gives a detailed snapshot of the MAC professional development plan. This chapter defines the program evaluation plan components supported with evidence.

Appendixes

The appendixes include sample materials from our MAC instructional planning, professional development organization tools, and data collection resources to inform success of the program and encourage systemic change.

REFERENCES

Carr, J. F., & Harris, D. E. (2001). *Succeeding with standards: Linking curriculum, assessment, and action planning*. Alexandria, VA: ASCD.

City, E. A., Elmore, R. F., Fiarman, S. E., & Teitel, L. (2010). *Instruction rounds in education*. Cambridge, MA: Harvard Education Press.

Common Core State Standards Initative. (2010). Retrieved from http://www.corestandards.org

DuFour, R., & Marzano R. J. (2011). *Leaders of learning*. Bloomington, IN: Solution Tree Press.

Hoy, W. K., & Tschannen-Moran, M. (1999). Five faces of trust: An empirical confirmation in urban elementary schools. *Journal of School Leadership, 9,* 184–208.

Lewis, C., & Hurd, J. (2011). *Lesson study step by step: How teacher learning communities improve instruction*. Portsmouth, NH: Heinemann.

Lewis, C., Perry, R., & Murata, A. (2006). How should research contribute to instructional improvement? The case of lesson study. *Educational Researcher, 35,* 3.

Sahlberg, P. (2015). *Finnish lessons: What can the world learn from educational change in Finland?* New York, NY: Teachers College Press

Takahashi, A., Watanabe, T., Yoshida, M., and Wang-Iverson, P. (2005). Improving content and pedagogical knowledge through kyozaikenkyu. In P. Wang-Iverson & M. Yoshida (Eds.), *Building our understanding of lesson study.* Philadelphia, PA: Research for Better Schools.

Tarter, C. J., Bliss, J. R., & Hoy, W. (1989). School characteristics and faculty trust in secondary schools. *Educational Administration Quarterly, 25*(3), 294–308.

Watanabe, T., Takahashi, A., & Yoshida, M. (2008). Kyozaikenkyu: A critical step for conducting effective lesson study and beyond. In F. Arbaugh & P. M. Taylor (Eds.), *Inquiry into mathematics teacher education* (pp. 139–142). San Diego, CA: Association of Mathematics Teachers Educators.

I

ORGANIZATIONAL PRACTICE

1

Multi-Age Framework

A Support System for Collaboration and Analysis

Teachers in a multi-age learning community school sit at extended lunch meetings for two hours discussing the things that went well and the tasks that seem to be a challenge for them during the day. These meetings are part of the MAC PLC collaborative conversations that take place once per week. Diane, a teacher for the "Detectives" (7- and 8-year-old learners), complains that her lessons are not accommodating her multi-age learners. She struggles with moving from the grade-level textbook scope and sequence to a standards-based approach. She asks other teachers how they are planning for so many developmental levels in the math and reading classroom.

Some teachers share that they designed curriculum maps early in the school year with the Common Core State Standards. A few of the teachers mention that they are trying to use a variety of strategies in lessons to accommodate individual needs of each learner. Some say that they use fluid grouping and differentiated methods, but they do not feel confident in the implementation. Diane reaches out to the principal to ask for help. She asks if there is a framework to assist teachers.

This type of situation is not surprising. In a multi-age classroom, each learner is on an individual developmental path. It is possible to have the mature 7-year-old and the average 8-year-old in the same classroom. Because learners are so different, teachers need to understand how to present a rigorous curriculum to all students. A teacher should begin by understanding the rationale (the why) for multi-aging, what multi-age means, gain insight into the philosophy and belief system, and gain knowledge of the practices. Shared collaboration with other educators is the appropriate support that makes this diverse classroom work for 21st-century needs.

WHY MULTI-AGE STUDENTS?

Goodlad and Andersen (1987) argued that a rigidly graded educational system is not designed for student development. In the graded system, a student follows an identical learning cycle with no room for diversity of the learner to grow. Goodlad believed that a multi-age learning setting is appropriate, rather than the graded system, for reason that students are given the freedom to develop at a pace that is optimal for their needs. If we consider Goodlad's ideas for the 21st-century schools, he stated in an interview the following:

> I think that there's no point in the schools continuing to be largely sources of information because it's all out there, available to children. It's a matter of helping them to organize information, make judgments, and so. However, there's very little of that going on in schools—not because teachers wouldn't like to teach that way—but, that's not what tests test. (Stone, 1999)

This multi-age program considers Goodlad's perspective and develops these ideas in a concrete manner. Students organize information and gain new knowledge that connects to the 21st-century needs.

SCHOOL OF CHOICE

The school reform political climate today focuses on *schools of choice* and building effective school environments. Multi-age classrooms integrate instructional models that are including individualized, personalized, and differentiated learning. These terms are defined as the following (Zmuda, Curtis, & Ullman, 2015):

- Individualized learning: the student controls the pace of the topic and controls when to demonstrate mastery
- Personalized learning: the student actively pursues authentic, complex problems that encourages inquiry, analysis, and discovery
- Differentiated learning: selects from a range of content, process, or product options; tailors instruction based on learner's needs

This multi-age program integrates a *school of choice* agenda by creating a unique school niche that is marketable to families. What this means is that parents can now move their children to schools that are located out of the catchment areas or district zones. Parents can shop for the best school that meets their children's needs. Parents have the option of sending their children to schools that are not based on the factory model.

Parents can select to enroll their children in a multi-age school with an agenda that concentrates on achievement that best meets the needs of the learner without disrupting the mandates of the curricula. It is an agenda that targets the individualized and personalized needs that each learner must build on to accomplish success from the educational system. This school focuses on one's own prior experiences, background knowledge, and cognitive capabilities.

Research supports the evolving roles of the student during instruction. According to Piaget (1953), schema refers to organized knowledge, experience, and expectations about some aspect of the learner's world. A student should build on schemata, mental structures created through one's experiences, with people, objects, events, and actions to obtain and acquire new knowledge (DiMaggio, 1997). Vygotsky (1962) explained that interactions with knowledgeable adults, imitation of learner modeling, and encouragement to move the learner to the zone of proximal development or potential level, are important factors in the learning process. These constructs are integrated into this multi-age framework.

WHY PRACTICE? WHAT DOES RESEARCH SAY?

The main purpose for using multi-age classrooms are educational and pedagogical, according to Veenman (1995), and are based on the assumption that teaching should be tailored to match each student's individual needs and differences (Finegan, 2001).

More recently, Proehl, Douglas, Elias, Johnson, and Westsmith (2013) discovered that students in multi-age classrooms exhibit improved social-emotional benefits (e.g., increased leadership in the classroom, fewer disciplinary incidents, and greater respect for classmates). Veenman (1995) unveiled other cognitive and noncognitive benefits of multi-age such as younger students observe, emulate, and imitate older children, and older students share expertise with younger students.

Since multi-age classrooms tend to make greater demands on teachers (e.g., ability of teachers to differentiate their teaching), the work of educators in professional learning communities (PLCs) increases the capacity of teachers to assist students to achieve academically (Bezzina, 2008; DuFour & Marzano, 2011; McLaughlin & Talbert, 2010).

Teachers work collaboratively to reflect on practice, examine evidence, and make changes to improve the teaching and learning processes (McLaughlin & Talbert, 2006).

These ideas foster a sense of ownership for teachers, and assist with creating teacher teams (DuFour, 2004; DuFour & Marzano, 2011).

Tomlinson (2014) proposes that educators look at teaching and learning in a way that moves away from the term "one size fit all." Tomlinson mentions that all students need to be seen as individuals with differing interests, background knowledge, and learning styles. Teachers need to make accommodations for each learner and differentiate curriculum.

Curriculum should make connections with students' prior knowledge and interests, and flexible groups should be organized to assist with meeting students' needs. Assessment should be ongoing to help teachers understand what students know or do not understand. These are important factors for the success of multi-age classrooms.

WHAT DOES IT MEAN TO "MULTI-AGE" STUDENTS IN A CLASSROOM?

This multi-age learning environment is responsive to the developmental needs of students. It is an active student-centered classroom that has many real-to-life experiences that have a variety of materials and resources to make rigorous curriculum come alive for students. These classrooms are best achieved by creating a diverse setting by integrating two or three grade levels together. Many teachers that are trained in multi-age programs are convinced that this kind of learning is best for children. Each learner works at his or her own pace.

When a school decides to multi-age learners in classrooms, this decision is based on a belief system (a philosophy) with very specific practices. These ideas are integrated into a quality and effective multi-age framework (Bingham, Dorata, Mc-Claskey, & O'Keefe, 1995) discussed in the following chapters of this book. The framework includes the following:

- Child-centered learning means that attention is focused on making decisions for each child based on a developmental context.
- Active learning is necessary for all children to learn—all children must be involved in the learning process using concrete materials, real-to-life experiences, and learning and interacting with other students. Conversations between students in a classroom support learning. Students learn to become independent thinkers and decision makers through these types of learning experiences.
- Belief that developmental diversity supports developmental learning for all students. Mixing ages assists students to learn at their own pace because the students learn from each other and work at their own level of understanding.
- Communities of Practice target groups of learners that share a passion for learning in what they do and when they learn how to do it better as they interact regularly (Wenger, McDermott, & Snyder, 2002).

Practices in a multi-age classroom (Bingham et al., 1995) integrate the following:

- Demonstrate knowledge of best practices for teaching content, concepts, and skills in multi-age classrooms using curriculum mapping and design strategies.
- Apply quality strategies such as collaborative behavior, fluid (flexible) grouping, and differentiated learning in classrooms.
- Integrate quality instructional practices: process writing, reading with informational text and literature, problem-based mathematics, hands-on science investigations, project-based social studies, and interdisciplinary thematic units.

- Use appropriate strategies to target the needs of English-language learners (ELLs).
- Construct a record-keeping system for tracking individual progress.
- Align formative assessment strategies to lesson objectives ongoing in each lesson.
- Design learning center tasks to reteach, instruct, and enrich individual learning.
- Communicate with parents and administrators ongoing regarding multi-age class events.
- Revise a grading report system to be more authentic to a multi-age setting learning environment.

As with Diane's situation at the beginning of this chapter, teachers in multi-age classrooms value how to respond to the individual or personal learning needs of each child at the student's developmental level. Diane will understand that it is easier for a teacher to observe a learner as an individual in this multi-age learning setting because grade-level expectations are not imposed.

Most importantly, the class environment is a learning community that becomes a "family" atmosphere that integrates the concept of a community of practice because children and teachers spend many hours together supporting and celebrating the growth of all learners.

According to Wenger (1998), a community of practice defines itself by binding educators and learners together into a social group that focuses on what matters for students. It also has members of the community sharing a set of communal resources such as routines, words, and the way of doing things. These resources give meaning to all actions of the day's events.

This multi-age community is a joint venture that encourages mutual accountability for improving the teaching and learning processes to improve achievement for all learners. Neighborhoods are formed in school buildings that connect classrooms as a large family for learning.

There is continuity for students to learn from year to year because children remain together with the same teacher for more than one year. This is a real plus for the teacher because he or she knows the child and what the child's capabilities are. In multi-age classrooms, a learner participates in many collaborative and cooperative situations, and as an outcome, the student feels comfortable sharing ideas and listening to other opinions.

Children have opportunities to help other children learn academic tasks, which assist learners to acquire knowledge and, for some, build quality leadership skills. Often an older child models management routines to acquaint students of the learning community with rules, routines, and lesson expectations. ELLs have many opportunities to share ideas using visuals and materials and they listen to others explain ideas.

Children with special needs blend into the community of learners because everyone is working at different levels with a variety of instructional materials. It is important that teachers understand just how to make this learning community a positive experience for all learners.

SNAPSHOT OF STUDENT-TO-STUDENT INTERACTION

The mathematics lesson objective is focused on the topic of place value and rounding three-digit numbers to tenths and hundreds. The "Investigators" (9- and 10-years-old) are working in groups, using place value materials and number lines to understand if they should round up or round down. This concept is difficult for some students. A 9-year-old child scratches his head and yells over to a 10-year-old boy that understands the problem "Hey, I don't get it! Can you help me?" The 10-year-old boy moves over to the 9-year-old and says, "Sure, I know what to do. You move this number up because it is over 5. Do you see that?" The 9-year-old boy reviews the materials and says "Okay, I think I get it now!"

This is just one kind of scenario that we often see as a natural process in a multi-age learning community setting. Students become teachers and leaders and help other students learn. This type of situation assists the teacher in the classroom because students take on a peer tutor role for other students. A student helping other students is an excellent way to understand how to become a leader. These leadership skills are lifelong learning skills for all students.

HOW ARE CHILDREN GROUPED?

The multi-age learning community places students purposely in classrooms to learn side-by-side with classmates that are more than one year apart in chronological age. The configuration of placing students together can range from two chronological age groups to possibly three chronological ages. The decision for a multi-age configuration in a school is based on the needs of the school community considering the number of students in an age group, space, class size, and the resources available.

All classrooms are grouped heterogeneously in nature. What that means is that a second and third grade classroom does not have the most advanced second graders combined in a multi-age classroom with the least advanced third graders. Sample variations of multi-age class configurations that work, are listed in table 1.1.

Variations of grouping multi-ages depend on the perspective of addressing the needs of each age group. For example, some multi-age schools find that 5-year-old learners have needs that require attention to adjusting to school life—napping during the day and gaining an introduction to academic skills. In this configuration, the 5-year-old children visit other classrooms in the neighborhood for only certain events. Sometimes, 5-year-olds integrate with the 6- and 7-year-olds during writing

Table 1.1. Sample Multi-Age Class Configurations

Multi-Age Configuration: Two Age Groups	Traditional Configuration	Multi-Age Configuration: Two or Three Age Groups	Traditional Configuration
3- and 4-year-olds	Nursery	3- and 4-year-olds	Nursery
5- and 6-year-olds	Grades K, 1	5-year-olds	Grade K
7- and 8-year-olds	Grades 2, 3	6- and 7-year-olds	Grades 1, 2
9- and 10-year-olds	Grades 4, 5	8-, 9-, and 10-year-olds	Grades 3, 4, 5
11-, 12-, and 13-year-olds	Grades 6, 7, 8	11-, 12-, and 13-year-olds	Grades 6, 7, 8

workshop sessions and interdisciplinary units of study. It is not unusual to see 6- and 7-year-olds working together in math and reading workshop and sharing time in the neighborhood during the learning center block with the 8- and 9-year-olds.

An important point to understand is that multi-age classrooms are not two grades placed together for one or two years only because of a population bulge. Neither is it a "combined" class in which separate curricula for each grade is taught. Such strategies for grouping multi-ages undermine the learning community school model (Bingham et al., 1995) and, as a result, teachers and parents become uneasy about the school program.

A school system that undertakes an instructional change for multi-age learners considers the impact on students, teachers, administration, and parents. As with Diane's concerns, teachers find instructional practice and pedagogy different from what they are used to from the past and they only have minimal preparation for implementing the new multi-age ideas. Students are unfamiliar with the new classmates and the new curriculum that integrates content and resources without following a textbook series.

Parents do not have the background knowledge of this new way of schooling. Administrators support teachers' uncertainty, frustrations, and concerns and respond to students and parents' reactions to the new multi-age program.

MAC FRAMEWORK: THE SUPPORT SYSTEM

How do schools change instructional practices to meet the needs of multi-age learners? The framework that is integrated in the MAC program connects to the following support system: Instructional Core and Practice, Vision Action Plan, Professional Learning Community, Instructional Rounds, and Lesson Study. The components for this framework follow next.

Instructional Core and Practice

When considering how to change instructional practice, teachers in the MAC program are considering the instructional core and the roles of teacher, student, and the influence of curriculum being taught. The instructional core model is a helpful framework to consider when intervening in the instructional process with the goal to improve the quality and level of student learning. The instructional core model in (see figure 1.1) (City, Elmore, Fiarman, & Teitel, 2010) has three components that are interrelated: teacher, student, and the interaction of the multi-age curriculum.

According to City et al. (2010), there are principles of the instructional core that should be considered when making instructional change for school improvement: student learning occurs only as an outcome of improvements with the multi-age curriculum, teacher's knowledge, and student engagement. It is important to note that if a teacher changes any element of the core, he or she must change the other two areas of the core or the outcome of new instructional practice will not be successful. For example, students in the "Detectives" classroom (7- and 8-year-olds) are given the number sentences, 4 × 3 = 12 and 12 ÷ 4 = 3. The teacher asks students to discuss the relationship between multiplication and division using these examples.

Rhonda, a 7-year-old, and Jack, an 8-year-old, share their solution by saying "They all have the same numbers, you just switch them around." Since the previous day's math lesson included that students construct arrays as models to show the concepts of the multiplication sentences, the teacher was expecting students to generate answers using arrays to show the concepts and relationships for this problem. But that did not happen. The teacher should have realized that if you can't observe

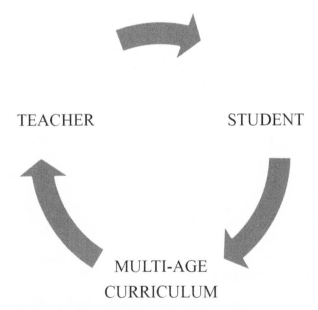

TEACHER   STUDENT

MULTI-AGE
CURRICULUM

Figure 1.1.   Processes of Instructional Core: Roles of Teacher, Student, and Curriculum

change in the core, then learning did not take place. To get students to understand these concepts the teacher retaught the concepts using other strategies.

Tasks that students are asked to do by the teacher predict performance of what learners can and cannot do. In this multiplication example, the students did not understand the concept and re-teaching was needed. The teachers and students learn to do the work by doing the work. According to the instructional core model, teachers should continue to analyze, predict what will happen, and then evaluate the learning situation so that learning can take place for each student.

All teachers in the MAC program are trained to design and implement quality multi-age curriculum. During this process, teachers look carefully at the Common Core State Standards for three consecutive grade levels that connect to the classroom age groups. For example, a teacher of the "Detectives" (7- and 8-year-olds) plans a math lesson on geometry. The teacher is trained to select the following Common Core State Standards (2010) to connect to plan curriculum for a geometry lesson using three grade levels:

Grade 2: Recognize and draw shapes having specified attributes, such as a given number of angles or a given number of faces.

Grade 3: Solve real-world and mathematical problems involving perimeters of polygons.

Grade 4: Apply the area and perimeter formulas for rectangles.

Considering the math content from the standards, in this situation, the teacher decides to teach perimeter concepts to the multi-age students and provide appropriate materials and resources.

For example, during the perimeter lesson, the students are told by the teacher that the number of units around a shape is its perimeter. The teacher shows one side of a square and labels it a "unit." The teacher asks each student to work with a partner to investigate how many different shapes can be made with five squares. Student partners (a 7-year-old and an 8-year-old) are directed by the teacher to count how many units they find around the shape to find the perimeter of each shape. The partners are given five squares and graph paper to solve the problem.

To extend the thinking level of the task, students are asked to find the smallest perimeter of a shape they create and justify why it is the smallest. Larry and Joy state, "We found six different shapes and three have 12 units and three have 10 units." Juan and Ree share, "We found 12 different shapes and they all had a perimeter of 12."

⌐⌐

It is important for the teacher to keep in mind that the instructional task is what the students are asked to do—not what the teacher thinks students are asked to do or what the Common Core State Standards say students should do. In this lesson, the teacher expects that students will find the appropriate perimeter for each shape by counting the units of each square using appropriate hands-on materials.

Some students count units that were included in the area of the shape. But, some students have difficulty with the task. Based on the instructional core model, if the teacher does not observe that students understand how to find perimeter, then understanding the concept is not there and reteaching is necessary. It is important for the teacher to realize that if you can't see it, then students do not get it.

This instructional core process is embedded in the MAC program because it assists teachers in understanding how to improve instructional practices. When teachers first go through the process of new learning, they are concerned with what the benefits of using the instructional core will be for the learners. This process needs to be explained and modeled for the students numerous times.

The next section of this chapter focuses on support system strategies that encourage shared leadership throughout the program. The elements for program support include creating a shared vision plan, developing Professional Learning Community (PLC) teams, and establishing instructional rounds and lesson study groups. In chapter 9, these share leadership elements will be supported with data from multi-age program practices in schools.

Vision Action Plan

How do we make it happen? Success is measured not by the performance of individual teachers, but by the performance of all school members, as a whole (McDonald, 1996). Vision action planning is a process that assists to move the innovation of the multi-age program to a high level. Success of the program depends on effective planning and facilitating the planning cycle between teachers and the administration (Glickman, 1993; Hall & Hord, 2001).

The school team begins by developing a vision action plan that addresses practical elements such as goals and objectives, timelines of events, budget, and consideration of resources needed in order to facilitate the new program structure. The committee establishes goals and observable objectives to measure what the program will look like when all program components are being successfully implemented. It is important to always consider that issues may arise during the change process and that the committee should be flexible (Zmuda, Kuklis, & Kline, 2004).

The vision action plan in table 1.2 is a sample plan for a multi-age program. This is a plan that gives some ideas on the beginning planning process of transforming governance from a traditional school program to a multi-age learning environment.

As in the sample vision plan, the focus is on developing multi-age classroom configurations, PLCs, and scheduling appropriate block time for teachers and administrators to have conversations around collective endeavors. Poor planning can damage a school. On the other hand, thoughtful planning can bring together a successful school environment. Staff should have an understanding and given clear

Table 1.2. Sample Vision Action Plan for a Multi-Age Program

Mission Statement: The mission is to develop communities that are academically excellent and welcoming, that enable students to be lifelong learners and good citizens of the world.

Vision: Design and implement multi-age program to meet the needs of the 21st-century student: problem solver, collaborator, critical thinker

	Action to Be Taken	Participants	Time Frame	Assessment
Goal: Governance of MAC				
Objective				
Example: Create configuration for a multi-age setting	Organize grade levels into multi-age neighborhoods	Principal, teachers, district	Ongoing	Observe how each neighborhood functions—use teacher survey
Objective: Create teams for multi-age PLC planning and discussion	Organize grade levels into multi-age neighborhoods	Principal, teachers, district	Ongoing	Observe how each PLC plans and collaborates—use journal reflections
Objective: Develop schedule for multi-age setting that integrates planning and implement phases.	Develop schedule	Principal, teachers,	Ongoing	Review schedule for lower and upper school
Objective: Establish appropriate resources to carry out program design	Collect resources	Principal, teachers, district	Ongoing	Review resources
Objective: Establish appropriate planning time	Planning time	Principal, teachers	Ongoing	Plan schedule
Objective: Delineated time for grade-level mandates	PLC Meetings	Principal, teachers	Ongoing	Schedule for meeting
Objective: Develop multi-age curriculum using Common Core State Standards	PLC Meetings	Principal, teachers	Ongoing	PLC Meeting Schedule

(continued)

Table 1.2. *(Continued)*

	Action to Be Taken	Participants	Time Frame	Assessment
Objective: Increase parent communication	PLC Meetings	Principal, teachers	Ongoing	PLC Meeting Schedule
Objective: Integrate Reading Workshop Components—interactive shared reading, close techniques, scaffold approach, flexible groups, literature circles, writing process, independent conferences	PLC Meetings	Principal, teachers	Ongoing	PLC Meeting Schedule
Objective: Math workshop—mini lessons, problem-based learning,	PLC Meetings	Principal, teachers	Ongoing	PLC Meeting Schedule
Objective: Interdisciplinary planning—based on school theme (two times or more)	PLC Planning Meetings	Principal, teachers	Ongoing	PLC Meeting Schedule
Objective: Application of formative assessments, portfolio for all students	PLC Planning Meetings	Principal, teachers	Ongoing	PLC Meeting Schedule
Integrate Instructional Rounds	Instructional Rounds Schedule	Research Group	Three times per year	Instructional Rounds Data
Integrate Lesson Study	Lesson Study Planning Time	Research Group	Three to four times per year or when needed	Lesson Study Data

direction of the shared vision and reality of transforming into a multi-age program before planning begins.

SNAPSHOT OF VISION ACTION PLANNING WITH STAFF

Ellyn, Brett, and Angel, teachers in the School of Arts, begin the work of the day by asking: what do we expect our school system to have in place before we begin the school year in September? They quickly agree that the vision action plan priorities are to configure students into multi-age classrooms, organize PLC teacher teams, and find ways to schedule meeting time. Angel announces to the team "Now that I have the opportunity to make sure that the vision plan is connected to the 'real work' of teachers, I am not sure if I know how to make this happen." They think about how they can direct the school to transform successfully into a multi-age environment.

They begin by creating objectives on how to begin the school year with the new program. They decide it is most important to consider how to select the configurations of each classroom. Do they combine two or three grades? They consider the student population and they look to see how many students they have in each grade. They also consider room availability and the number of teachers on staff. After conversations for about an hour the team determines that the school program can accommodate two grades in each multi-age classroom. Then, they think of how to select PLC teams based on the multi-age configurations. That decision is made based on which teachers will plan and collaborate daily.

They decide that Ellyn, the teacher of the Picasso class (grades K–1) will be on a PLC team; Bret, the teacher of the Monet class (grades 2–3); Angel, the teacher of the Van Gogh class (grades 4–5) will be a team; and the teachers for the Rembrandts' classes (grades 6–8) will be a team. The last objective that they must discuss for the day is how to schedule time for teams to schedule meetings. They generate and record some ideas, but they decide to take the information to the other staff members, so that others can have input into the vision planning process.

This teacher team had conversations for the first time and they collectively established ways that some specific objectives of the action plan can be operationalized. These conversations validated that a school program is a complex, living system with purpose. These teachers realized that they were very much a part of the change process in the school and that they were able to take ownership for the development of the new program.

MAC Professional Learning Community

The basic premise of MAC PLC teams is that educational leaders and teachers can and should be working together to collaborate and to cooperate on planning lessons, developing assessments, studying curriculum, and otherwise improving student learning (DuFour, Eaker, & DuFour, 2005; McLaughlin & Talbert, 2006). It is important that collaboration occurs. This happens when teachers and administrators share ideas about instructional strategies and techniques, make decisions about instructional issues, and generate ideas that improve and enhance learning for all multi-age students.

The framework for MAC PLC has three major ideas: sharing practices, review of data, and a focus on student learning. The overarching goal of MAC PLC includes a constant creation of new knowledge within the organization and the aim of putting it into practice by using collaborative inquiry and reflection (Hord, 2004; Stoll & Louis, 2007). The following characteristics by Kruse, Louis, and Bryk (1995) drive the framework of the MAC PLC intervention: (1) shared leadership, (2) focus on student learning, (3) focus on teacher quality, (4) support interaction among teacher colleagues, (5) encourage a collaborative culture, (6) emphasize shared mission, vision, values, and norms in a school community, and (7) reflective dialogue.

The educational leader's role in managing and implementing MAC requires shared leadership. The leader takes charge by educating and empowering teachers and serves as an advocate for the reform effort. The Common Core State Standards are at the center of all conversations of leaders and teachers to plan and provide quality instruction. Through interactions among teachers, professional relationships are developed that encourage teachers to share ideas and expertise, learn from one another, and help other colleagues.

Through the deprivatization of practice, teachers are encouraged to open their classrooms for teachers to observe classroom strategies (Roberts & Pruitt, 2009). Reflective dialogue is a process when educators across classrooms have conversations which focus on teaching behaviors and learning outcomes to encourage teachers to discuss their teaching practices. An important characteristic of PLCs is that these groups share values and norms in the community. It is important that educators of MAC reach agreement about which quality program components shape the appropriate behaviors of the professionals in the school.

SNAPSHOT OF A MULTI-AGE PROFESSIONAL LEARNING COMMUNITY

The neighborhood in the multi-age school has a school wing that has a classroom of "Explorers," the 5- and 6-year-olds, the "Detectives," the 7- and 8-year-olds, and the "Investigators," the 9- and 10-year-olds. The teachers in this neighborhood work as a team. They are part of the PLC and they are scheduled to plan together, discuss standards-based curriculum, share curriculum maps, and analyze student performance. Teams have numerous responsibilities.

Teams may schedule the day together by all doing math workshop and reading workshop at the same time or plan an interdisciplinary theme together.

Some teams schedule center time together and children can choose activities in any one of the four classrooms during this time slot. Sometimes, teachers offer Author's Workshop by allowing learners to move in and out of classrooms. A Reader's Theater is offered once per week. This is when the four classrooms extend out into the corridor. The families of the community of learners gather in the center hall to share poems, stories, and informational logs.

The principal facilitates MAC PLC meetings to show appropriate support wherever needed. Curriculum is discussed on an ongoing basis during PLC time. This is a time when teachers discuss how standards are being addressed for all students. Teachers are allowed to share students' work to make decisions.

Most importantly, team conversations are reflective in nature. Teachers discuss the positive and negative aspects of the teaching and learning process. Teachers take time to visit other teachers' classrooms to see successful implementation of program strategies. The educational leader becomes part of the group to assist with planning instruction and sharing data results.

MAC Integrates Instructional Rounds

The important issue of understanding if practice is effective in a multi-age classroom is to observe what is going on. The instructional round is defined as a process that allows principal, teachers, and other professionals to systematically develop ways to solve school problems. An instructional round is about observing classrooms to learn from the school's own practices and develop plans for taking steps that are likely to lead to sustained improvement over time.

Before the instructional round is conducted, the leadership team discusses a problem that has surfaced in the school program. The problem might be that the scores on the reading test are below average performance. Roberts (2012) labels this problem as the *problem of practice.*

This problem allows school members to consider an area of weakness in a school program that needs to improve and then, find ways for improvement. The team creates a problem of practice and then moves around to classrooms to see how instructional practices are applied. During an instructional round, leaders enter classrooms to look to see what teachers know and are doing, what students are doing and saying to each other, and what type of lesson is being implemented.

In a qualitative manner, the team collects data on what exactly is being observed. The question the team asks is "What do we see?" while recording descriptive information that eventually transforms into patterns and relationships. Three to four times per year, the principal and leadership team move through classrooms to look at what is going on. The instructional Rounds Process, adapted from City et al. (2010), follows this framework:

- **Generate the Problem of Practice:** The problem of practice is one concern that surfaces during instruction. This problem of practice is posted during the rounds session so that observations are focused on just how to improve practice.

- **Observe:** Observe a classroom in action and look at interactions of what the teacher is doing, what the students are doing, and what curriculum is being offered, considering the multi-age framework.
- **Describe:** Each team member describes what he or she observed using non-judgmental language. Copious field notes considering the school's vision for multi-age practice are recorded by each team member.
- **Analyze:** The team debriefs about what they see across classrooms. The team analyzes field data and then codes data into categories and patterns that relate to the multi-age learning environment.
- **Predict:** The team predicts what the students are learning in this multi-age learning environment. Are the students doing what they need to do to be successful?
- **Next Level of Work:** From the data, the team discusses and decides what the school should do to improve practice and provide necessary professional development.

SNAPSHOT OF INSTRUCTIONAL ROUNDS IN ACTION

The school team uses the instructional rounds to observe if the multi-age classrooms are functioning effectively. Once every month, a school team of leaders, teachers, and professional development coaches enter a classroom to conduct an Instructional Round. The team is asked to block out everything they assume is going on in the class. This is harder than it sounds because educators always have preconceived notions of what should be happening in the classroom. They observe what the teacher and students are doing and consider what exactly the teacher is doing with the content.

There is always a problem to consider when doing rounds. It is often called the "problem of practice." The "problem of practice" for this round is to observe multi-age students in a classroom and consider how students understand the expectations of the multi-age classroom. It is a broad objective because it is early September and the teachers just arrived back to school after receiving professional development on the application of multi-age components at a Summer Academy. The team enters the "Detectives" classroom with paper to write on. The team takes notes as they look on as to what students are doing during the lesson. The teacher gives a quick introduction of the student expectations of the lesson. Then, the lesson unfolds with a teacher presentation on main idea and details in a reading passage and then students work in pairs to find the components applying the strategies: reading through once, chunking paragraphs and circling academic vocabulary. The pairs are asked to record the main idea and the supporting details on a storyboard which is later shared in a whole class group discussion.

After the classroom observation, the team regroups back in the conference room. The group processes the data collected from the classroom observation by allowing each person to spend time looking over his or her own notes. Then, the team members write their data on sticky notes. This gives each person time to reflect on the observation and think of events that seem most closely related to the "problem of practice."

Another purpose of these sticky notes is that they can be organized in a variety of ways to allow the group to tell a story about what they observed in the classroom. Then, the team places the sticky notes on a chart paper posted on the wall. With the group, each person helps each other think about what they did see/hear that makes them think that. The group members read each sticky note aloud to the group.

After about ten minutes of reviewing the descriptive data together, the group decides to classify the notes into categories: teacher, students, content of lesson. This way group notes can be changed at any time. However, the notes are categorized based on the "problem of practice." Then, the team reviews the grouping of sticky notes and predicts what students were learning in this classroom. The next level of work for the team is to make suggestions for the next step. The debrief session does not solve the problems, but rather give direction for the next instructional round session. The instructional round process is not an evaluating tool that will punish school members, but is a reflective tool to gain insight on how to continue to improve instructional practice in the multi-age classroom.

Multi-Age and Lesson Study

Lesson study is a collaboration of professional educators who plan, observe, and reflect on lessons. It originated in Japan as an embedded professional development agenda that improves educational systems (Lewis, 2002). Lesson study is defined as the study of teaching practice by discussing lessons that a team of educators have planned and observed together. One teacher implements the lesson that was created by the lesson study group and another teacher observes and then reteaches the lesson with improved methods. The concept of lesson study seems simple and obvious: if you want to improve education, get teachers and educational leaders to study the processes of teaching and learning in classrooms, and then devise ways to improve them.

In a multi-age environment, educators conduct lesson study as part of the school professional development program. Teachers, the principal, and members of the leadership team in a school, review areas that need improvement. Lesson study adds to the research-based framework for strengthening and encouraging data-driven decision making and debriefing sessions by using a research group to oversee the MAC lesson process.

The cycle of planning, observing, reflecting on, and revising a lesson leads to increased knowledge of content and instruction, increased ability to observe students, and strengthen a community of collaborators. For example, if teachers are struggling with the implementation of a multi-age mathematics lesson, then the lesson study team will meet and discuss how to improve a mathematics lesson by designing a quality lesson. Then, one teacher volunteers to teach the lesson and the lesson study team visits and observes the lesson in action.

During the lesson study, the team looks to see what the students are doing during the lesson—do learners understand what they are doing, and if so why, and if not, why not. After the implementation of the lesson, the lesson study team debriefs on what they saw during the lesson. They discuss the strengths and the areas that need to be improved. The team then, confers on a new lesson considering how instruction should be improved. The cycle of lesson study continues. Lesson study is discussed in later chapters with documented conversations during debriefing sessions.

SNAPSHOT OF A LESSON STUDY SESSION

The MAC team found that test data show that students are struggling with problem-solving skills in the "Collaborators" classroom of 11- and 12-year-olds. A lesson study team designed a quality lesson together to find a way to improve instruction. As an outcome, the lesson study team gathers to observe a lesson on problem solving with a connection to real world issues. The team includes teachers from other neighborhoods, the principal, and the professional development coaching members. The teacher of the lesson from the Collaborators decides to give students the following problem. For example, we are setting up for a family reunion in the park. We have five hexagon shaped tables. If one chair is on each side of each table, how many people can sit at the tables? The teacher gives anticipated solutions to the lesson study team before the lesson observation begins. The anticipated solutions are: $5 \times 6 = 30$, $6 + 6 + 6 + 6 + 6 = 30$, $(6 + 6) + (6 + 6) + 6 = 30$. The teacher knows that some students in this multi-age group will need an extended thinking task, so she creates the following:

Oh no! It started raining and we have to move tables inside, but we have less room. Now how many people can sit at these five tables? Anticipated solutions were given as $5 + 4 + 4 + 4 + 5 = 22$, $15 + (3 + 4) = 22$, $30 - 8 = 22$, $(5 \times 4) + 2 = 22$. The objectives that teachers hoped for were that students developed algebraic habits of thinking, find calculating shortcuts to solve problems, develop equivalent expressions for a given problem, and become problem solvers using open-ended problems.

Students worked in collaborative heterogeneous groups of 11- and 12-year-olds and were given math materials of hexagons to manipulate and graph paper for recording solutions. The lesson study team moved around the classroom to view what students were doing to solve the problem. After the lesson, all student groups shared the group results. After the lesson, the lesson study group moved into a meeting room to discuss what they observed. Did the students understand the problem? Were they able to make connections? Was there rigor in the lesson geared toward understanding the problem-solving process? The lesson study group moved away knowing much more about the instructional core: what the teacher is doing to create rigor and include problem solving, what the students are doing when solving problems, and how the curriculum standards were connected to the learning process.

This close look at a lesson is preparing principals and teachers to continue to reflect on how instructional practice should change to meet the needs of all learners in the program. Lesson study is just one effective strategy to assist with the improvement of instructional practices.

Principal Support

A principal should not ignore that a teacher, such as Diane, needs help with implementing the multi-age classroom. Diane believes that multi-age students in classes is an effective way to teach students. However, this teacher verbalizes that she is nervous early in the implementation process of setting up a multi-age program. One concern is that the teacher does not understand how to plan for diversity in the classroom. She is unsure of what materials should be used for the developmental levels in mathematics and reading. From the onset of the program, a support system should be organized that provides ongoing professional development inside and outside the classroom. More information on how to support teachers in this program will follow in other chapters.

EDUCATOR'S REFLECTION

Educators and researchers (Fullan, 2001; Hall & Hord, 2001; Hord, 2009) know that change in a school system is a process, not an event. School leaders are pressured to find an immediate solution, but, they realize early, the change process is a complex issue. This chapter reinforces that collective accountability and implementing an innovation is necessary. It also provides a support system that includes tools to develop and revise the school elements for changing a traditional program into a multi-age learning community.

The tools to assist the change team in a school include considering a vision action plan, reviewing the instructional core to improve practice, organizing a PLC with teachers, observing classrooms with instructional rounds and improving on lesson implementation with lesson study. This chapter introduces these strategies and later chapters will continue to connect these ideas with real classrooms. In chapter 2, the roles of teacher teams (PLCs), instructional leader, and teacher leader are defined and connected to the strategies that encourage the multi-age school reform agenda.

APPLICATION OF CONCEPTS FOR ALL SCHOOL SYSTEMS

- All school programs consider how to strengthen collective accountability. All school members should become leaders in their school, working to achieve the desired results.
- Teachers rethink teaching practices and student expectations of student outcomes considering the curriculum. Considering the instructional core will improve instructional practices.
- A shared vision and action plan is developed by all school members.
- Professional development is embedded into everyday tasks. PLCs, instructional rounds, lesson study, and evaluating the instructional core are strategies that are applied to make improvement and change in a school program.
- Most importantly, teachers and educational leaders need time to reflect on practices and have time to develop and apply new ideas. These new ideas to improve school programs are based on data collected through conversations, observations, and what students know and can do.

REFERENCES

Bezzina, C. (2008). The journey of a Maltese Catholic church school. *Management in Education, 22*(3), 22–27.

Bingham, A. A., Dorata, P., McClaskey, M., & O'Keefe, J. (1995). *Exploring the multiage classroom.* York, MA: Stenhouse Publishers.

City, E. A., Elmore, R. F., Fiarman, S. E., & Teitel, L. (2010). *Instruction rounds in education.* Cambridge, MA: Harvard Education Press.

Common Core State Standards Initative. (2010). Retrieved from http://www.corestandards.org

DiMaggio, P. (1997). Culture and cognition. *Annual Review Sociology, 23,* 263–287.

DuFour, R. (2004). What is a professional learning community? *Education Leadership, 61*(8), 6.

DuFour, R., Eaker, R., & DuFour, R. (Eds.). (2005). *On common ground: The power of professional learning communities.* Bloomington, IN: National Education Service.

DuFour, R., & Marzano R. J. (2011). *Leaders of learning.* Bloomington, IN: Solution Tree Press.

Finegan, C. (2001). Alternative early childhood education: Reggio Emilia. *Kappa Delta Pi Record, 37*(2), 82–84.

Fullan, M. (2001). *Leading in a culture of change.* San Francisco: Jossey-Bass.

Glickman, C. D. (1993). *Renewing America's schools.* San Francisco, CA: Jossey-Bass.

Goodlad, J. I., & Anderson, R. H. (1987). *The nongraded elementary school.* New York, NY: Teachers College Press.

Hall, G. E., & Hord, S. M. (2001). *Implementing change: Patterns, principles, and potholes.* Boston: Allyn & Bacon.

Hord, S. M. (Ed.). (2004). *Learning together—leading together: Changing schools through learning communities.* New York, NY: Teachers College Press.

Hord, S. M. (2009). Professional learning communities: Educators working together toward a shared purpose. *Journal of Staff Development, 30*(1), 40, 43.

Kruse, S. D., Louis, K. S., & Bryk, A. (1995). An emerging framework for analyzing school-based professional community. In K. S. Louis & S. D. Kruse (Eds.), *Professionalism and community: Perspectives on reforming urban schools* (pp. 23–42). Thousand Oaks, CA: Corwin Press.

Lewis, C. C. (2002). *Lesson study: Handbook of teacher-led instructional change.* Philadelphia, PA: Research for Better Schools.

McDonald, J. P. (1996). *Redesigning school: Lessons for the 21st century.* San Francisco, CA: Jossey-Bass.

McLaughlin, M. W., & Talbert, J. E. (2006). *Building school-based teacher learning communities: Professional strategies to improve student achievement.* New York, NY: Teachers College Press.

McLaughlin, M. W., & Talbert, J. E. (2010). Professional learning communities: Building blocks for school culture and student learning. *Voices in Urban Education, 27*, 35–45.

Piaget, J. (1953). *The origins of intelligence in children.* New York, NY: Basic Books.

Proehl, R. A., Douglas, S., Elias, D., Johnson, A. H., & Westsmith, W. (2013). A Collaborative Approach: Assessing the Impact of Multi-Grade Classrooms. *Catholic Education: A Journal of Inquiry & Practice, 16*(2), 417–440. Retrieved from http://digitalcommons.lmu.edu/cgi/viewcontent.cgi?article=1732&context=ce

Roberts, J. E. (2012). *Instructional rounds in action.* Cambridge, MA: Harvard Education Press.

Roberts, S. M., & Pruitt, E. Z. (2009). *Schools as professional learning communities.* Thousand Oaks, CA: Corwin Press.

Stoll, L., & Louis, K. S. (Eds.). (2007). *Professional learning communities: Divergence, depth, and dilemmas.* Glasgow: McGraw-Hill.

Stone, S. J. (1999). A conversation with John Goodlad. *Childhood Education, 75*(5), 264.

Tomlinson, C. A. (2014). *The differentiated classroom: Responding to the needs of all learners.* Alexandria, VA: ASCD.

Veenman, S. (1995). Cognitive and noncognitive effects of multigrade and multi-age classes: A best-evidence synthesis. *Review of Educational Research, 65*, 319–381.

Vygotsky, L. S. (1962). *Thought and Language.* Cambridge, MA: MIT Press.

Wenger, E. (1998). *Communities of practice: Learning, meaning and identity.* Cambridge, MA: Cambridge University Press.

Wenger, E., McDermott, R., & Snyder, W. M. (2002). *Cultivating communities of practice: A guide to managing knowledge.* Boston, MA: Harvard Business School Press.

Zmuda, A., Curtis, G., & Ullman, D. (2015). *Learning personalized: The evolution of the contemporary classroom.* San Francisco, CA: Jossey-Bass.

Zmuda, A., Kuklis, R., & Kline E. (2004). *Transforming schools: Creating a culture of continuous improvement.* Alexandria, VA: ASCD.

2

Collaborative Inquiry

Roles of Principal, Teachers, and Teacher Leaders in a Multi-Age School

The principal of the newly formed School of Literacy Learning Academy has problems getting her teachers to collaborate and plan curriculum on a yearly basis. Most teachers work on planning lessons based on what the textbook tells them to do. The administrator tries to convince the staff that when multi-aging students are in a classroom, they should not follow each grade-level textbook and teach to each grade curriculum.

The principal encourages teachers to plan and try to collaborate and communicate with one another on what they are planning to teach. The principal emphasizes that Common Core State Standards should play an important role in this planning process. However, most teachers in this school struggle with making these connections. Collaboration is difficult when teachers do not have much time to have conversations with others.

The teachers continue to ask for the principal to designate others in the school building that they can rely on to get their questions answered. The principal becomes overwhelmed with how to move ahead with teacher concerns. The principal tries to visit classrooms and attend meetings on a regular basis. This principal understands that she needs to support teacher efforts the best way possible.

This situation in schools happens all the time. Teachers and principals are collectively responsible for providing the most effective way to obtain student achievement on high levels. Teachers need time for planning and discussing lessons. After all, teachers are made to be the curriculum planners because the textbooks in some subject areas are now only supplemental to what should be taught in the classrooms.

The multi-age curriculum requires a considerable amount of time for planning so that standards are targeted appropriately and all learners get what they need based on developmentally appropriate practice. In chapter 1, the framework for supporting a successful multi-age program was discussed. In this chapter, we look at the specific roles of principals, teachers, and teacher leaders during collaborative processes.

PRINCIPAL'S ROLE IN A
MULTI-AGE SCHOOL ENVIRONMENT

What effect does the principal have on teaching and student achievement in a multi-age school environment? Research tells us that the school leader must be effective in his or her actions if a school community is to succeed (DuFour & Marzano, 2011). However, as was discussed in chapter 1, according to the instructional core, the actions and behaviors of the principal do not directly affect students because the school administrator usually does not present instruction. The principal's influence on student achievement passes through teachers. Teachers give instruction to students and therefore have a direct effect on student achievement (DuFour & Marzano, 2011; Marzano & Waters, 2009; Marzano, Waters, & McNulty, 2005). So, how does the principal make an impact on the professional practice of the teachers in the multi-age program?

In a multi-age program, a shared leadership approach is supported. A school leader cannot approach a multi-age school environment with a traditional perspective. Traditionally, the principal is unable to reach all teachers with vision ideas. In a shared leadership environment, the principal organizes a PLC to encourage team collaboration among teachers and the administration. This framework easily targets the Responsibilities of a Leader that have been outlined by theory and research (DuFour & Marzano, 2011; Marzano et al., 2005).

This structure allows the principal to interact with each school team on an ongoing basis. Important concepts that should be considered for leading a multi-age program focus on the areas of governance, culture-building, curriculum, instruction, and assessment.

As explained in the leadership components in table 2.1, the principal has an important role and should be a strong advocate for the multi-age program. Not only is it the responsibility of the leader to share vision and expertise, but it is also his or her responsibility to communicate how teachers should make the necessary changes to improve instructional practices to increase student performance.

Fullan (2014) points out that there are two major changes in schools that influence the principal role: Common Core State Standards and continuing digital innovations. These particular demands in education have challenging implications when added to the need to transform the school program into a collaborative culture for a multi-age program design.

The principal needs to market the program to the school community whether it is for parent groups, district supervisors, teachers, or the community at-large. When selling the program to teachers and the community, the leader should be very knowl-

Table 2.1. The Leader (Principal) Role in a Multi-Age School Environment

Marzano's Leadership Roles	As Applied in a Multi-Age School Environment
Change Agent	Willing to make revisions in the school that are very different from the status quo that includes management of routines, multi-age grade configuration, schedules, curricula, and assessment factors.
Communicator	Addresses all teachers, students, and parents' concerns about the program implementation. Creates rewards of performance on all levels.
Culture Builder	Fosters a shared vision, builds community with a culture of collaboration, and establishes clear goals that should be carried out for the multi-age community of teaching and learning
Intellectual Conversation Facilitators	Encourage intellectual conversations among teachers, teacher leaders, and the community through PLCs, Instructional Rounds, lesson study groups, and application of concepts using theory to practice for a multi-age learning environment.
Curriculum, Instruction, and Assessment Leader	Models and supports curriculum, instruction, and assessment because the leader stays current on new applications.
Resourcer	Provides professional development, materials, technology, and resource books to teachers for implementing the program successfully.
Assessment and Data Analyst for School Improvement	Reviews data and assessment strategies on an ongoing basis to evaluate student performance with teachers and suggest improvement.
Outreach Spokesperson	Spokesperson for school on all levels.

edgeable on program theories and concepts (Elmore, 2000; Fullan, 2014; Reeves, 2004), so that the leader may deal with any concerns that may surface.

PRINCIPAL AS CHANGE AGENT AND INSTRUCTIONAL PLANNER

A principal is the first person in the school environment to assist teachers in the new instructional planning process. First, the leader recognizes that he or she must encourage the teachers to cope with instructional change. Administrators and teachers who work in isolation will most likely not change instructional practices. Teachers and administrators should be engaged in collaboration and collective inquiry. This is a systematic process in which teachers work together to impact classroom practices which lead to positive outcomes for students and the school environment (DuFour, DuFour, Eaker, & Many, 2010).

With the redesign of a classroom into a multi-age setting, instructional practice must change in order to make effective improvement. School leaders in this environment focus on the "how" of leadership to understand how to lead the school into a collaborative culture (Spillane, 2006). This multi-age program focuses on a distributed leadership model that emphasizes the way school leaders and teachers interact, how artifacts from the school environment influences their interactions, and how the roles of leaders and teachers evolve over time.

Also, it is important to note, when applying this shared leadership model, a person may be a leader in a certain situation, and that person may be a follower in another event. Leadership is a fluid phenomenon that happens ongoing in the school building between the principal and the teachers (English, 2011).

Research connected to school practice is effective when collaborative teams form between administration, teacher leaders, and teachers to make such connections. Collaborative cultures do not just happen in a school—but, these collaborative environments (as in PLCs) must be schoolwide endeavors or the culture will not change (Hargreaves & Fullan, 2012). Therefore, teams must communicate and have meeting time to discuss how to work together to change classroom practices to meet the needs of diverse learners.

A principal assists teachers by considering the following elements when encouraging teachers to make instructional changes (Showers & Joyce, 1996):

- Make connections to the vision action plan.
- Present why the research-based strategy should be applied.
- Model the strategy.
- Collaborate with peers on how to integrate the skills successfully in the classroom.
- Support one another during the teaching process.
- Continue to review assessment data to improve instruction for each student.

The administrator creates an environment that is supported through ongoing reflective dialogue. Reflective strategies that work well in multi-age programs with teachers and teacher leaders include PLCs, instructional rounds, and lesson study groups—strategies introduced in chapter 1. These structured processes elicit conversations among the school leader and teachers about lesson appropriateness and what each student should be doing during the lesson that is observed.

These shared leadership strategies also allow principals to benefit from the collaborative team structures. No one principal has all of the knowledge, skills, and expertise to carry out all responsibilities of a school leader. It is important to enable others in the school environment to take the lead in identifying and solving problems (DuFour & Marzano, 2011). The teacher leaders in a school program assist the principal with school reform efforts. The need for a strong team in a school is cited again and again in research (Marzano et al., 2005; Sergiovanni, 2005; The Wallace Foundation, 2013).

SCHEDULE TIME FOR COLLABORATION

The most difficult element for effective implementation of the multi-age program is finding the time to allow teachers to collaborate with other teachers. Some effective suggestions are the following:

- Group teachers whose students have the same specialty subjects such as art, music, or physical education at the same time.
- Schedule lunch and a specialty subject side-by-side two times per week.
- Create a whole group activity that two or three classes can participate in at the same time.
- Offer a writing workshop or reader's theater for a large group of students.
- During faculty meetings leave time for PLC groups to meet.

The main issue is to build the collaboration time into the schedule before the school year starts so that the schedule is carved into everyday school activities.

PRINCIPAL AS SUPPORTER

The principal as supporter has a very important role of modeling curriculum planning, modeling lessons, discussing the resources necessary for the implementation process, and providing continuous suggestions on how each teacher might take the next step in the change process. The principal visits classrooms on a regular basis to view how lessons are implemented.

The walkthrough process is an important tool to gather information on what is being taught in classrooms each day. The walkthrough only takes about 3–5 minutes for a principal to move into a class to observe just what is going on. This is an informal observation process. The principal does not evaluate the teacher—rather he or she looks for one particular objective to assess during the walkthrough.

For example, in a multi-age class, teachers use a variety of pedagogical strategies such as teacher directed lesson, scaffolding, fluid grouping, cooperative teams, independent work, and problem solving. The principal may walkthrough to see how one strategy is implemented. After the walkthrough the principal will conference with the teacher to give feedback on the observation.

SNAPSHOT OF A PRINCIPAL IN A MULTI-AGE SCHOOL

Rosa is a principal that realizes that innovation and risk-taking are two important elements in her shared leadership role in the school. She is willing to revise the grade configuration for multi-age needs because she believes that developmentally appropriate practice should be considered during instructional practice. She has reconfigured the traditional grade system into a multi-age configuration. She has one grade at each level. She looks to see what the multi-age class would look like if she decided to combine two grades (i.e., PK 3 and 4s, K–1).

Does she have enough of one age group to achieve a balance with the other age group? Does she need to combine three age groups? Can she make this multi-age grade configuration work across the school program?

Rosa communicates the philosophy of the program to her teachers by allowing her staff to participate in creating a shared vision action plan that is based on the needs of the school environment. From this vision, all teachers understand the direction of the school based on clear goals and objectives. Rosa, as leader, is always moving around the building having ongoing conversations with the learners, other teacher leaders, and teachers. She visits classrooms during walkthrough sessions considering a purpose and sometimes participates in lessons with the learners.

Rosa enjoys teaching writing, so as an outcome, she takes time out of her busy schedule to teach a mini lesson during writing workshop. This principal also encourages the lesson study model by requesting that her team conduct it at least two or three times per school year. Rosa enjoys joining the lesson study research group so that she can give constructive input on how lessons may become more effective for student learning.

Rosa rotates the position of leading a lesson study session with other teachers. Some projects might include connecting the inquiry process in a 9- and 10-year-old social studies unit using a new digital technology process or looking closely at how 7- and 8-year-olds write informational text on a science topic of their choice. She participates in curriculum mapping early in the school year to support the teachers' ideas and she makes note of materials and resources that might be needed to carry out instructional themes and topics.

Although Rosa transfers her leadership role to the teacher teams and teacher leaders during PLC meetings, she still attends group meetings and reviews data with the committee to evaluate student areas of improvement. She also reviews the rubrics that are generated during team meetings to understand just what conversations took place. Rosa stays abreast of issues and supports and communicates ideas to assist with the transformation of the multi-age school.

COLLABORATIVE INQUIRY: THE ROLE OF TEACHER IN A MULTI-AGE SCHOOL

How great is it for teachers to take time for intensive professional growth and learning right in their own school building? This embedded professional development opportunity that includes teacher teams such as PLCs, instructional rounds, and lesson study, creates a strong learning community. This school environment generates enthusiasm and provides professional development among staff. Collaborative inquiry during teacher team meetings is defined as an investigation of teacher and leadership practices when considering instruction to improve student learning (Teitel, 2013). This inquiry process is necessary.

Collaborative inquiry is a three-phase process. This process includes the following: discussing and recording effective instructional practices that have been tested, reflecting on issues that may lead to new ideas, and reflecting on experiences and data collected in the classrooms. It is recommended that the principal allow teacher teams and teacher leaders to control the process (DuFour & Marzano, 2011; Marshall, 2005). It should be an informal process owned by teachers.

Teams are very important because if teachers work in teams, they plan together. Teachers in MAC are encouraged to plan curricula together, implement units and lessons, and have ongoing conversations on assessment and student improvement.

Some neighborhood teams schedule times during the day so that all classes are doing mathematics and reading workshops at the same time. This allows teachers to move some students into other reading or math groups in the neighborhood to target the needs of learners. Many of the teachers become active participants not only in the PLC collaboration, but also in discussion during principal walk-through sessions and in the instructional rounds process.

The role of the principal should be to check on teachers to make sure they are not just simply going through the motions superficially, rather than develop a true collaborative culture focused on improving teacher instruction and student learning. The principal helps teacher leaders and teacher teams define and own their collaborative processes.

Hargreaves and Fullan (2012, 2013) stated that a professional capital vision should be applied when focusing on developing teacher teams. This process builds up the expertise of teachers individually and collectively so that the teaching and learning process improves. This is done by considering human capital (talent of teachers); social capital (the collaboration process of the teacher team); and the decisional capital (allow teachers to use expertise to make appropriate decisions and judgments about learners). This professional capital vision model is integrated into the MAC program processes. The concepts will integrate into chapters 3–9.

Collaborative inquiry groups help teachers and principals become learners through purposeful collaborative efforts and conversations in which student performance is the focus. These teams also design and implement effective curriculum plans based on conversations, observations, and the review of data. Therefore, if a principal asks for a prepackaged multi-age curriculum (which happens in schools often), this school leader ignores just how a quality curriculum is collaboratively designed.

RUBRIC TO GUIDE COLLABORATIVE INQUIRY FOR TEACHERS

The MAC collaborative teams use a formative assessment rubric to guide the performance of each team meeting. Teachers use a rubric to monitor collaboration and suggest goals and objectives of each session.

Roles of the team members during the meeting are assigned prior to the session (e.g., facilitator, scribe). A meeting agenda is distributed prior to meeting day and was reviewed by team members from a previous session. Collaboration at the meeting is assessed through observation of teacher participation, sharing of expertise, professionalism, and goals. Teacher leaders and members of the team look to see if all teachers are sharing ideas, making suggestions based on expertise, are supportive and cooperative, and how the team decides on the next step toward improvement.

For example, some questions that surface during a team meeting are: Did the facilitator send the agenda prior to the meeting to all participants? Did the conversations target just how to observe the problem of practice in classrooms? What is the next step to take for this action item? The following rubric in table 2.2 is a sample

Table 2.2. Rubric for Team Collaboration

Problem of Practice: _____

Roles of the team	Roles were clearly assigned at the meeting. Notes:	Rating: 0 (low) to 5 (high)
Participation	Every member of the team shared ideas. Notes:	Rating: 0 (low) to 5 (high)
Sharing of expertise	Each member discussed teaching methods and strategies, and professional development needs. Notes:	Rating: 0 (low) to 5 (high)
Professionalism	Members compromised, were democratic, reached consensus, were engaged, cooperative, and supportive. Notes:	Rating: 0 (low) to 5 (high)
Goals	Data was presented to support improvement, materials were presented to show curriculum and assessment to improve instructional practices, and a clear action plan was designed for moving to the next step. Notes:	Rating: 0 (low) to 5 (high)

rubric that was constructed so that the team is able to rate the performance of the team meeting from 0 to 5, to confirm that the teachers accomplished what they set out to accomplish.

One teacher responded to the use of the rubric by saying, "We all came to the meeting with different ideas. However, once we created the rubric, it gave us a clear focus on how to run the meeting in a coherent and productive manner." The team process and rubric are important elements to assist teachers and principals with improving multi-age curriculum and the implementation processes in classrooms.

THE ROLE OF THE TEACHER LEADER IN A MULTI-AGE SCHOOL ENVIRONMENT

Teacher leadership has been around for quite a long time. Formerly, teacher leader roles included serving as department chairs, participating as members of curriculum teams, or just assisting the school administrator, whenever necessary. This type of teacher leader role was limiting because teachers only took on a representative position for an administrator, rather than a role of teacher leader that encourages change in a school environment.

As an outcome of the recent surge for performance accountability, school systems are considering that qualified teachers should take on nonsupervisory school-based roles as teacher leaders—a strategy to improve teachers' instructional practices and enhance student achievement (Mangin & Stoelinga, 2010).

This role gives the teacher leaders an opportunity to share instructional expertise, provide school-based professional development, co-plan with curriculum mapping, model standard-based multi-age lessons, visit classrooms, and promote effective practices with other teachers. In the multi-age school environment, these teacher leader roles are necessary because all participants in this program need a person or other educators that can be trusted to discuss program components ongoing during the implementation process.

The teachers at the School of Literacy Learning Academy knew they needed a few teachers that they could go to for input when they needed their questions answered. In this school, the principal is not always the leader. Teacher leaders are selected by the administration and teachers.

For example, the School of Literacy Learning Academy found a need for one teacher leader in the lower school and one for the upper school. Barth (2013) mentions that principals cannot run a complex school environment alone. These teacher leader roles are based on the distributed leadership process where teachers take on the decision-making process to advocate for a shared school vision. One way to get teachers invested in what they are doing is to let them sit at the table and take on a leader role of making decisions. This decision-making process in the MAC program encourages teacher buy-in of the program and it helps teacher leaders to advocate for the shared culture that is transforming through the collaborative framework.

Research tells us that there are specific elements to consider when selecting a teacher leader (Mangin & Stoelinga, 2010). A teacher leader must have the following characteristics: have an understanding of content knowledge in all subject areas, practice as a reflective practitioner, enjoy collaborating with others, and build trust with all teachers and administrators. According to Lieberman and Miller (2007), the teacher leader takes on the roles of researcher, scholar/collaborator, and mentor. These teacher leader characteristics are embedded in the MAC program.

As researcher, the teacher leader creates new knowledge from direct teaching practices. The advantage to this critical inquiry process is that teachers improve instruction in the classroom, gain new knowledge through this reflective practice, and this process extends to the whole school redesign. The teacher leader, as scholar, makes one's work public in some way, allows others to critique the ideas, and shares it with others so that other teachers can build on the strategies. The teacher leader feels more efficacious about teaching because it builds on expertise; credibility develops in the field and influences the school program.

The teacher leader as coach is at the center of re-culturing the school program. This teacher leader influences others by collaborating and studying practice in other classrooms and encourages ongoing improvement for teaching and learning within the school (Levenson, 2014; Lieberman & Miller, 2007).

Principals should realize that it is important to maintain a professional culture for teacher leaders. This means that the principal should support and trust teachers as they make thoughtful decisions. Principals need to establish conditions so that teacher leaders can excel: allow them to have time to have conversations with other colleagues on an ongoing basis; give data so that teacher leaders can diagnose student learning needs; give opportunities for incentives to learn from colleagues in other classrooms and other schools, and continue to emphasize that decision making is based on teamwork (Hargreaves & Fullan, 2012).

Principals must oversee that all teacher leaders work in a nonthreatening environment. If a parent or another colleague does not show respect to the teacher leader, the administrator needs to conference with these groups to gain necessary acceptance of the teacher leader and also help the leader to reflect on ways to merit the respect of peers. School schedules must also accommodate the meeting times for the teacher leaders to interact with other teachers whether during planning time, teacher class meetings, and one-on-one interaction.

A school may have more than one teacher leader on staff. The teacher leader is based on the individual school program. However, there are commonalities to teacher leader roles in the MAC program. Teacher leader roles range on a continuum from an informal to formal level. On an informal level, this teacher leader is a teacher researcher that carries out action research plans, participates in rounds, and is an instructional team member that will not hesitate to make changes. On the formal level, this teacher leader is a coach, certified teacher, workshop leader, data team leader, and co-teacher leader in a school (Levenson, 2014). In the multi-age school environment, the selection of the appropriate teacher leader is crucial.

The MAC program continues to gain ideas from national programs such as the Peer Assistance and Review (PAR) and the two Boston-based models—the T3 teams and the Boston Teacher Leadership Resource Center. All programs have been carefully designed to strengthen teaching and learning through teacher leadership models.

Significant commonalities from such programs filter into the MAC teacher leader ideas: teacher leaders affirm the importance of experience, professional knowledge, and collaboration; teacher leaders need the background to work with adults, politics, and culture of the school; teacher leaders need to be prepared to take criticism from colleagues; neither the principal or the teacher leaders are expected to make changes by themselves, and; most importantly, teacher leaders should be passionate about their work (Levenson, 2014).

SNAPSHOT OF A TEACHER LEADER

Katie has been selected as a teacher leader for the School of Literacy Learning Academy. Katie has been teaching for approximately 10 years and has taught most grades K–8. Since the school transformed into a multi-age environment, Katie works at using a variety of teaching strategies to target individual needs of her students. Her specialty area is in English language arts. She uses a variety of books to teach her content area. She differentiates lesson content by using workshop directed lessons, small group work, literature groups, scaffolding techniques, and independent conferencing. Katie reflects on data analysis to revise her approach to teaching students on an ongoing basis.

Katie is also a teacher leader with a role to lead the other teachers in collaborative practice that is effective for multi-age students to learn on high levels. She is the teacher leader in her PLC team. This community is deliberate in what they do and how they do it. Katie assists PLC members to address challenges by examining issues both inside and outside the multi-age classroom. This teacher leader shows other teachers how to use summative and formative data to inform the work of the team. The team focuses their work on reviewing data from common assessments in the classroom and by sharing ideas about how to improve instructional practice to meet the needs of learners based on what the data reveals. The team looks carefully at the state test to see what areas students need help with.

Katie leads curriculum planning with colleagues to design themes for multi-age concerns and directs teachers on how to review curriculum on a yearly basis. Additionally, another teacher leader in the school leads a research group on lesson study, to look in classrooms to see just what students are doing during a specific lesson. And, just about every two months, Katie is asked to participate in an instructional round process to look at "problems of practice" and find some ways to make improvements during a debriefing session that she directs.

EDUCATOR'S REFLECTION

Many of the strategies discussed in this chapter help educators to consider how to take the next step for improving student learning. In particular, collaborative inquiry during teacher team meetings (PLCs) discussed more fully in chapters 3–6, assists with the collaborative investigation of how to improve teacher practices to encourage student achievement. Collaborative inquiry is a process that helps teachers to determine curriculum topics and the effectiveness of the instructional practices.

The role of the principal is to assess the performance of teams to make sure the focus is on improving instruction. As they collaborate with school leaders, they observe that the administrator uses walkthroughs to observe if team agendas are applied in classrooms and to give ongoing feedback. A rubric guides the team meetings to confirm that meeting discussions are coherent and productive. It is important that the principal in MAC follows a framework from Responsibilities of a Leader generated by Marzano et al. (2005). This framework is a guide to encourage the principal to be a change agent, communicator, culture builder, supporter, and spokesperson. Also, the principal makes connections to the vision action plan ongoing, models ideas, and collaborates with staff.

The new teacher's role as a team member is essential for making collaborative inquiry sessions work successfully in a school building. In the MAC program, MAC PLC teams plan and have ongoing conversations about curricula. The teachers continue to have conversations in order to identify and take the next steps for school improvement.

The most important role in a school today is the teacher leader position. A teacher leader is a role in the MAC program that shares instructional expertise and promotes effective practices with other teachers, administrators, and parents. The teacher leader is selected from the school staff based on outstanding performance in the classroom. The teacher leader is a good support person that all teachers can trust and rely on when they are confused or just have questions.

APPLICATION OF CONCEPTS FOR ALL SCHOOL SYSTEMS

All school programs should encourage the following:

- Collaborative inquiry is a process to investigate how to improve instructional practices.
- The new teacher's role includes a collaborative element with other colleagues.
- Teacher teams (PLCs) are essential for allowing time for conversations on how to plan curriculum and discuss how to increase student achievement.
- A rubric to guide team discussions is available for use.
- Principals need to support teachers using walkthroughs to give effective feedback on instructional practices.

- Teacher leaders should have a role in school programs. Each teacher leader shares expertise and promotes effective practices with teachers, administrators, and parents. Teacher leaders are teachers that staff members can rely on when questions surface.

REFERENCES

Barth, R. S. (2013). Leveraging teacher leadership. *Educational Leadership, 71*(2), 10–16.

DuFour, R. DuFour, R., Eaker, R., & Many, T. (2010). *Learning by doing: A handbook for professional learning communities at work.* Bloomington, IN: Solution Tree Press.

DuFour, R., & Marzano, R. J. (2011). *Leaders of learning.* Bloomington, IN: Solution Tree Press, 62–63.

Elmore, R. F. (2000). *Building a new structure for school leadership.* New York, NY: Albert Shanker Institute.

English, F. W. (Ed.). (2011). *The sage handbook of education leadership: Advances in Theory And Practices.* Thousand Oaks, CA: Sage.

Fullan, M. (2014). *The principal: Three keys to maximizing impact.* San Francisco, CA: Jossey-Bass.

Hargreaves, A., & Fullan, M. (2012). *Professional capital: Transforming teaching in every school.* New York, NY: Teachers College Press.

Hargreaves, A., & Fullan, M. (2013). The power of professional capital: With an investment in collaboration, teachers become nation builders. *Learning Forward, 34*(3), 36–39. Retrieved from www.learningforward.org

Levenson, M. R. (2014). *Pathways to teacher leadership: Emerging models, changing roles.* Cambridge, MA: Harvard Education Press.

Lieberman, A., & Miller, L. (2007). What research says about teacher leadership? In R. H. Ackerman & S. V. Mackenzie (Eds.). *Uncovering teacher leadership: Essays and voices from the field.* Thousand Oaks, CA: Corwin Press.

Mangin, M. M., & Stoelinga, S. R. (2010). The future of instructional teacher leader roles. *The Educational Forum, 74,* 49–62.

Marshall, K. (2005, June). It's time to rethink teacher supervision and evaluation. *Phi Delta Kappan, 86*(10), 727–735.

Marzano, R. J., & Waters, T. (2009). *District leadership that works: Striking the right balance.* Bloomington, IN: Solution Tree Press.

Marzano, R. J., Waters, T., & McNulty, B. A. (2005). *School leadership that works: From research to results.* Alexandria, VA: Association for Supervision and Curriculum Development.

Reeves, D. B. (2004). *Assessing educational leaders.* Thousand Oaks, CA: Corwin Press.

Sergiovanni, T. (2005). *Strengthening the heartbeat: Leading and learning together in schools.* San Francisco, CA: Jossey-Bass.

Showers, B., & Joyce, B. (1996). The evolution of peer coaching. *Educational leadership, 53*(6), 12–16.

Spillane, J. P. (2006). *Distributed leadership.* San Francisco, CA: Jossey-Bass.

Teitel, L. (2013). *School-based instructional rounds: Improving teaching and learning across classrooms.* Cambridge, MA: Harvard Education Press.

The Wallace Foundation. (2013, January). *The school principal as leader: Guiding schools to better teaching and learning*. New York, NY: The Wallace Foundation. Retrieved from http://wallacefoundation.org/knowledge-center/school-leadership/effective-principal-leadership/Pages/The-School-Principal-as-Leader-Guide.aspx

II

CULTURE BUILDING

3

A Community of Learners

Building a Caring and Trusting Environment for All Students

John, the teacher in the Global Community Multi-Age School, has a conversation with the school leader about creating a caring school environment. John asks the leader, "How can I get my students to care about other learners during the school day? It doesn't look like that students get along well with each other. Also, the parents seem to be isolated from the tasks of the classroom. What does it mean to create a community of learners that includes all members in this learning environment? What can we do to make this a more caring and trusting learning environment?"

COMMUNITY OF PRACTICE IN A MULTI-AGE SCHOOL

What does community of practice mean for the multi-age school program? Wenger, McDermott, and Synder (2002) define members in this group to be participants of a school that share a set of problems and are passionate about this type of schooling. These same school members deepen their knowledge and expertise in multi-age programs to help to improve learning for all students. This is done in a multi-age school by implementing meaningful learning environments that emphasize effective learning situations for all students that encourage higher-level thinking, rigor, collaboration, and problem-solving settings. These programs also provide support through resources and remove any barriers in the school environment that might hinder the function of the multi-age program.

BUILDING A CARING AND
TRUSTING SCHOOL ENVIRONMENT

The first step for transforming a multi-age school into a community of learners is to build a caring and trusting environment. According to past research (Comer, Haynes, Joyner, & Ben-Avie, 1996; Meier, 1995), social and relational trust in schools help to build relationships that support school reform efforts. Bryk and Schneider (2003) define social elements, as the social relational exchanges that are generated from the school leader and between all school groups: teacher/student, teacher/teacher, and teacher/parents. Relational trust is defined as having all members in a school environment understand their roles of personal obligations and recognize the expectations of others.

Comer's School Development Project that integrated trust components showed that urban school staff and parents of low socioeconomic status improved student achievement (Comer et al.,1996). In a middle school in Harlem, Meier (1995) defends, that in her school, trust among teachers, leaders, parents, and students helped to improve middle school performance. What these studies indicate is that all participants remain dependent on their own actions and others, to achieve desired multi-age school goals. Trust elements are formed around the roles that participants have in the school.

As individuals in a school environment interact with one another, they are always concerned on how actions influence others (Bryk & Schneider, 2003; Kochanek, 2005). For example, in a multi-age school, the school leader encourages teachers to maintain a caring school environment that engage leaders, teachers, parents, and students in all community events inside and outside the classroom walls.

Teachers need support from the school leader by receiving appropriate resources for the learning environment and to assist with carrying out lesson tasks. Parents are asked to participate in activities and gain an ongoing understanding of what students are doing from day to day. Students are asked to support other students by leading students that need their help, by cooperating and collaborating with others, and by showing a sense of kindness to all.

When thinking about caring and trust situations in the multi-age school environment, we use four elements to discern the intentions of others in the learning environment: respect for all, competence, integrity, and personal regard for others (Bryk & Schneider, 2003; Kochanek, 2005).

Respect for all in the multi-age environment emphasizes regard for others during all school interactions. All participants become good listeners and respond to situations in an appropriate and supportive manner.

Competence is when a school member carries out the participant's role in a productive way—a teacher is competent based on student success; a leader is competent based on how school agendas are successfully implemented; a student is competent when working on learning to reach his or her potential level; and, a parent is competent for staying involved during homework and class events.

Integrity is modeled through implementing actions that consider what is in the best interest for school community members. Lastly, personal regard for others involves showing kindness to all (Bryk & Schneider, 2003; Kochanek, 2005).

BUILDING A NEW SCHOOL CULTURE

Improving school culture needs much more than changing the structure of schools (transforming governance, time use, and grouping). To succeed in building a new school culture, both new structures and a professional culture are elements to consider. Schools tend to improve when the focus is on student learning and a commitment to high expectations.

A successful school culture has the support for innovative ideas and reflective dialogue. Also, it is important to have a caring, trusting, and sharing group of teachers and staff that get along and have a shared mission and action plan that they have created in a collective way. This process helps all teachers and staff to take ownership to new ideas.

Research on re-culturing schools (Abplanalp, 2008) include enhancing curriculum and instructional practices and providing quality professional development for both teachers and students. How does a multi-age school initiate improvement? First, a school should have strong mission/vision statements that will encourage staff to initiate improvement efforts. Second, collegiality is encouraged among staff because this element is related to collaborative planning and decision-making efforts. Third, cultures with a strong focus on improvement are more likely to consider implementing new effective instructional strategies.

Finally, multi-age schools improve best when successes are recognized and celebrated ongoing through small collaborative ceremonies applauding both individual and group contributions (Abplanalp, 2008; Deal & Peterson, 2009).

MULTI-AGE LEARNING COMMUNITY TO REINFORCE CULTURE

Learning communities (DuFour, 2007) are used in the MAC program to reinforce the cultural elements for multi-age school success that include:

- Shared sense of purpose by establishing a mission and vision statement that encourages the multi-age philosophy.
- Teacher involvement in decision making during teacher team planning of curriculum mapping and thematic studies and for teacher leaders to support and collaborate with other teachers.
- Teams of teachers collaborate and work around effective instructional practices such as problem-solving groups, thematic studies, project-based learning, learning centers, and orbital studies (independent work).

These strategies are defined and discussed in greater detail in chapters 5–7.

Professional learning and development is ongoing in this multi-age program. The initial professional development cycle lasts for at least a 3-year period. This professional development framework is discussed in detail in chapters 1, 2, 8, 9, and 10. A sense of joint responsibility for student learning is embedded in the multi-age school environment because teachers and administrators continue to discuss and reflect on how to reach all students. Instructional rounds and lesson studies are conducted ongoing throughout the school year to discuss the norms of improvement. These strategies are discussed in other chapters in detail.

DEFINING SHARED CULTURE FOR TEACHERS

In the MAC program shared culture affects all aspects of the school environment. Shared culture fosters teacher productivity and effectiveness because the school culture creates a climate where continuous fine-tuning and refinement of multi-age teaching is supported by all colleagues. Informal conversations between faculty members are valued. These conversations integrate ideas about instructional practices and their shared commitment for making the program work for all learners.

Teachers, teacher leaders, and administration collaborate ongoing and work together. No one in the school environment works in isolation. Teacher leaders are always available to give suggestions and support any teacher or administrator. For example, in the Discovery School, a teacher leader supports a teacher by giving suggestions on how to implement a guided reading lesson on information text.

The teacher leader visits the classroom and observes just how the class teacher is implementing a guided reading small group session followed by debriefing with the class teacher on how strategies can improve in the lesson. Such a culture helps a teacher to overcome the uncertainty of his or her work and allows a teacher to constantly improve his or her craft.

DuFour (2007) stated that shared culture improves collaboration, communication, and problem solving. In MAC schools teachers are offered opportunities for the social and professional exchange of ideas. In the Literacy Academy, an inner city school that has a large population of ELLs, the school teachers and administrators meet for a book club once per month, after school hours. It is a social event where educators discuss book topics that may enhance their teaching. In particular, in one school, the staff decided to read *Professional Capital: Transforming Teaching* by Hargreaves and Fullan (2012).

The purpose of selecting this book was to identify how to become more effective in improving learning and achievement for all students and close the gap between those from advantaged and those from disadvantaged social backgrounds. The book club conversations center on professional exchange of ideas that enhance effective practices through professional problem solving. The educators discuss how to improve professional capital (expertise of staff), social capital (how to improve collaborative efforts), and decisional capital (how to make the right decisions for the learners).

DEFINING SHARED CULTURE FOR LEARNERS

A shared culture is known to promote innovation and school improvement (Deal & Peterson, 2009; Waters, Marzano, & McNulty, 2004). The MAC program embeds innovative practices and integrates new approaches in multi-aging classrooms. Multi-age students are always working together on projects with students of all ages. We do this to encourage change in schools to foster a quality environment so that all students learn at their potential levels.

This is why active learning environments are encouraged that target the needs of each student through hands on tasks; problem-based learning situations, real-to-life experiences, and leadership opportunities. For example, in the Discovery School, students in small problem-solving groups created a Project-Based Learning (PBL) unit for three weeks on designing a school environmental center. The question that guided the project was "How do we construct a functional environmental center in our school community?"

Small groups collaborated on researching other environmental centers to understand what components were needed for this project. They measured and planned a site outside the school building for the construction project. And, they designed a budget, a location, and added photographs to the proposal. A final proposal was presented to parents, staff, and community members. The students also included a video in their presentation to depict how an environmental center can be constructed in the school environment.

Educators in MAC programs are motivated and committed to the shared school environment because it has meaning, appropriate values, and a clear purpose to encourage high levels of student learning (Schein, 2004). The educators are motivated because ceremonies build a multi-age community and stories convey the meaning of the multi-age philosophy.

In multi-age schools, students' projects are displayed on walls in halls and classrooms. For example, in the hall in the lower school of the Discovery School, a large mural is displayed. This mural is painted by all children in the lower school based on the book *Life Story* (Burton, 2009). The learners read the book on the story of the lifecycle. It is easy to see trilobites and igneous rock in one area of the mural and metamorphic and sedimentary rock formations in another corner. The lower school created a musical about *Life Story* and performed for the school community and parents during an evening school event.

In the upper school, students become authors and share their books and poems during a refreshment session at a lunchtime period. And, all students are invited once per month to attend a *theater in the round* session where any student in the school may share a poem, an information text, or a short skit that they created during the month. They may also share a *leadership moment* where a student or students reflect on a special leadership role that made a difference in the school. These events in this positive shared culture influence the emotional and psychological orientation of the school. This multi-age learning environment creates an optimistic, caring, supportive, and energetic setting where all members feel comfortable.

SNAPSHOT OF LAUNCHING A MULTI-AGE SCHOOL LEARNING ENVIRONMENT IN A DISTRICT AND SCHOOL

District Level

"Do you think the multi-age learning environment will be a good model for teaching and learning in our district?" Ellie worried for the fifth time. As the deputy superintendent she had a personal stake in the success of the model. Her colleague John, the superintendent of the district, responded understandingly, "Sure, Ellie. We initiate this program for a few reasons: it is an effective way to teach and accommodate all children's needs; it helps with our district's funding issues; and, it is a good way to support school choice for those parents that are looking for a more effective way to teach their children." Ellie replied, "We can't mandate that each school in the district make the change from a traditional program to the multi-age learning setting."

"We can, however, introduce the concepts to all the district administrators and suggest that they think about how this model can help their schools flourish. We can offer to support an appropriate professional development program for any school in the district from an outside team at an administrator's meeting and again at a teachers' meeting."

School Level

"I think we need to help our diverse group of students learn on high levels," Ted explained to other teachers over coffee. "I happen to agree, but what can we do?" Jerry jumped in to say, "We all teach primary grades kindergarten through grade 3. Why don't we try to team up and combine the grades into a multi-age program? We can plan together, team teach, and make sense of what the students' needs are."

In regard to the district approach in the district-level snapshot or the teachers' approach in the school-level snapshot, change comes in many forms. To be effective with the change process it is important to have the appropriate support from the school system. The new program develops the kind of cohesion that lets participants in school systems support each other—and, hold one another accountable for their actions in their instructional improvement work.

CASE STUDIES OF SCHOOL ENVIRONMENTS

There are numerous schools that transformed into multi-age programs. The following case studies represent a sample of the kinds of schools that made the transformation.

Each case study is represented based on the school's background with emphasis on the purpose of the school, how the multi-age environment supports a caring atmosphere, and a description of the multi-age practices.

Case Study 1

Principal Amanda Davies oversees a K–5 school. The school is an urban public science/mathematics magnet school that received Federal funding. This school is an inner city school with a very diverse population. The school has three classes per grade level. In a K–3 corridor, four teachers are discussing how to target the needs of their students. The multi-age school program is labeled the "Exploratorium Learning Space."

The mission/vision is to enable each of the students to develop cognitive and metacognitive abilities, social skills, and science and mathematics concepts that will make students high-level thinkers and lifelong learners. There are three purposes for this multi-age program: children develop at their own pace; the program allows interaction and modeling among younger and older children; and, there is a strong emphasis on the integration of a science/mathematics interdisciplinary model. Children in this school receive a good foundation in using skills and content to stimulate higher-level thinking, problem solving, and collaboration.

During informal conversations in the faculty lounge, teachers discussed how to take the curriculum and make it an exciting program for their learners. This multi-age program grew out of teacher frustration of not being able to target the needs of all learners.

The teachers of one K–3 met often and planned a multi-age program that integrated science/mathematics workshop during a theme period labeled the "Discovery Workshop." There are two main strands in the program: a primary strand and an intermediate strand. Homerooms are labeled a name such as "Investigators," "Explorers," "Detectives," or "Voyagers" to alleviate inappropriate graded system labels such as grade 3, grade 4, and so on.

The organizational structure eliminates fragmented instructional time blocks. The workshops are presented three mornings per week for two hours for each session. Each teacher/facilitator presents an interdisciplinary hands-on workshop to multi-age children around a science/mathematics theme. All children in each strand attend each workshop by the end of the week. Mathematics and reading workshops are offered two mornings per week. Afternoons consist of writing workshop or special project-based seminars.

The principal of the program formed relationships with the teachers and parents early on when the program was initiated. She moved throughout the school interacting with teachers and students by visiting classrooms and becoming involved in the lesson tasks. She was supportive to teachers, by giving them materials for class lessons and projects. She was the "go-to person" when teachers had questions about curriculum and assessment strategies. She was easy to talk to and was often found in the cafeteria during early morning drop off, mingling with parents and conducting informal meetings to keep parents updated on the school events. Teachers describe this school leader as a caring person that they looked up to and imitated.

Case Study 2

The School of Investigation is a small charter school that struggles to keep the school doors open. Principal Diane has been the school principal for five years. She was directed by the School Board of Directors to consider transforming the school into a multi-age learning environment for a few reasons: the students' needs are addressed in a more specific manner when considering a rigorous curriculum and a caring and trusting learning setting; the school has limited funding and must combine grades to meet organizational commitments; and, the school connects to a highly competitive marketplace. This multi-age philosophy creates a market niche, a unique school identity. Families are now allowed to select such a school that is located out of the catchment area or zone of the district. These reasons make this school highly attractive to Board of Directors and parents.

This PK–8 school does not have many seasoned teachers. The novice teachers approach this multi-age school reform project as an opportunity to help students in their school perform better. Teachers realize that the student population is small and it is their job to create a school environment that will be more appealing to the families in the local area.

This School of Investigation is a school that emphasizes science concepts in all areas of the curriculum. Theme teaching and learning are organized around science topics. Students are encouraged to learn through real-to-life experiences that help them to concentrate on environmental issues and consider how to improve the natural community.

This school adapts to a multi-age program in a slow manner—each year the lower grades transform into multi-age classrooms. In the first year, the preschoolers, ages 3–4 were placed together and the kindergarten and first grade were placed together. In the second year, grades 2 and 3 merged together and grades 4 and 5 were placed together. The middle school grades 6, 7, and 8 stayed as a traditional setting with a focus on an interdisciplinary theme running through the program. The school leaders and teachers decided that this slow process to move to a multi-age school program was the best decision to allow for all school members to adjust to the new multi-age environment.

Homerooms were labeled by asking children to brainstorm ideas. As an outcome, the homerooms are "Birds" in PK 3–4, "Elephants" in grades 1–2, "Hippopotamus" in grades 3–4, and "Eagles" in grades 4–5. This environmental school integrates many local community field trips and events to assist students to investigate environmental issues.

Students explore the local water bodies to collect specimens of pond life. The learners take daily environmental walks in the neighborhood to observe and collect natural artifacts based on the changing seasons. All outdoor events allow students to perform as environmental scientists collecting data and analyzing information to improve community areas. Math and reading workshops meet each morning. In the afternoon, Environmental Workshop is offered twice per week and project-based interdisciplinary lessons are offered three times per week. Writing workshop is integrated each afternoon for 45 minutes at the end of the day.

The principal of the school encourages caring and trusting elements in the multi-age learning community on an ongoing basis. The principal encourages teachers to go to seminars and return to the school to present ideas learned during a monthly teacher workshop session. Teacher leaders are selected to support staff ongoing in classrooms and share ideas. Parents are invited into the classrooms to assist with lessons and share their own expertise with learners on an ongoing basis. Learners are encouraged to help other students in a variety of ways.

A "buddy" program allows learners to work with a buddy to share ideas, ask questions, and just be a friend. The teachers feel that this multi-age school learning community has a very positive atmosphere like a "family" relationship. Since it is a small school, everyone helps each other and collaborates on agendas because all participants have taken ownership to the vision of the environmental program.

SNAPSHOT OF A TYPICAL DAY FOR A STUDENT IN A MULTI-AGE COMMUNITY OF LEARNERS

Jamie is an 8-year-old girl in the multi-age program. She begins her day at 8:40 a.m. in a "Voyager" homeroom. She sits on a rug during meeting time recording personal thoughts and feelings in her journal. Today is a special homeroom for Jamie because she is one of the four children that will submit her journal to the teacher/facilitator for personal feedback. Then, she sits with a friend to share her personal ideas. Her friend Michael gives her comments about her ideas. Children in this group love to share ideas with each other because they respect everyone in the class. It is 9:00 a.m. on a Monday morning.

Jamie moves down the corridor holding a learning log in her hand to a science/interdisciplinary multi-age workshop. She is greeted at the meeting area by Ms. Robinson, teacher facilitator for this session. The children sit in a circle listening to the instructions before taking an excursion outdoors for an urban "Senses Walk." An activity always builds on the child's prior knowledge.

A brainstorming session begins with Jamie giving her personal definition of the word "senses" by explaining to her group the following: "senses, to hear, see, smell, touch, and taste are tools on our bodies that we use to observe the world around us."

Before heading out in the community, the teacher/facilitator takes children through a session on using their senses as tools for observing the environment. The children close their eyes and pay close attention to the sounds they hear. They open their eyes and then create a group tally chart of all the different sounds they can describe. Then, the children are asked to close their eyes and feel their fingertips. They are instructed to move their fingertips across the surfaces of various objects; their shirtsleeve, chair, and crayons. They are asked to describe the differences in texture of each object.

With their eyes still closed, they sniff a piece of paper, a pencil, and a crayon. They describe the noticeable differences of the objects. The children end the task by describing an object that catches their eyes using color, size, shape, and texture works. Jamie and her classmates now have the tools to make accurate observations in their community. Children divide into cooperative learning groups of four multi-age children. Each child in the group has a special job of either materials manager, leader, recorder, or timekeeper. They all understand how to cooperate with each other.

Jamie, as the materials manager of the group, hands out simple supplies needed for the excursion: paper, pencils, crayons, hand magnifiers, plastic bag, trip board, and a simple map of the area to be explored. Outside, Jamie's group makes rubbings of tree bark. The leader asks group members to collect found objects of different plant life. The recorder tapes city sounds on an audio recorder. All group members create sketches of the area explored. When the group returns indoors they make one big map of the area investigated. Each group's reporter describes the findings of the group and the materials manager reorganizes the materials and conducts a cleanup. Each child is given an opportunity to reflect on the outdoor task in a learning log.

Shortly before lunch, Jamie attends a mathematics workshop. Today Jamie is working with a multi-age partner on probability/estimation tasks. Partners receive a recording sheet with the numbers 2 through 12 going across the top and a pair of dice. Jamie is asked to predict which sums surface the most as she rolls and adds the numbers on the dice. Jamie and her partner Sam take turns in the group rolling and adding the dice. As each sum comes up an "x" is placed in the appropriate column. The task ends when one column is completed. The whole multi-age class comes together and shares their results.

As homework, Jamie takes her personal recording sheet and dice to see if she gets different results working at home with the facilitation of a parent. This activity allows Jamie to learn about probability and reviews her numerical concepts and shares what she knows inside and outside math class.

In the afternoon, Jamie attends writing workshop. The Voyagers and the Explorers collaborate in the corridor and classrooms. Two teachers team teach together to work with all student writers. The workshop begins with Mr. Adler presenting a mini lesson for approximately ten minutes on characterization using a literature book titled *Time for Ballet* by Geras (2003).

Mr. Adler introduces the book by stating that this is story of a young girl going to ballet class, practicing, and even overcoming preperformance jitters. The teacher mentions that "I will read aloud a few pages of the book and I want everyone to focus on the key details about the character."

The teacher models for the class how to create a character map outline and which elements make a character come alive in the book. He discusses the character actions, what the character says, where the character lives, and how the character interacts with others. Today, the teacher points out that the children should think about just how the character is a caring and trusting individual.

Following the mini lesson, Jamie returns to work on her own story that she has been developing for the past few days. Today, however, Jamie needs help with developing her character in her story. She moves to the rug area to confer with a classmate. Jamie reads aloud the draft and receives good feedback. Children love to share their ideas and expertise by giving feedback to other authors. Later in the week, Jamie is anxious to publish her work as a book by using the computer and creating a special handmade book jacket. Parents will be visiting for tea in two weeks and she needs to prepare for the author's presentation at the tea party.

Project-based independent projects are integrated at the end of the day. In keeping with the theme of the environment, Jamie and her friends decide to write a letter to the city's recycling organization to ask for help in starting a recycling project at their school.

At the end of the day, Jamie returns to homeroom, a grade-related group, to reflect on the day and the event, to organize her homework and plan for tomorrow. Homeroom, in the early morning meeting, and at the end of the day, allows for time when grade-related topics need to be discussed.

EDUCATOR'S REFLECTION

This chapter mentions some important elements that drive collaborative efforts in a multi-age learning community. The elements that build a caring and trusting environment are interwoven in all actions of the multi-age school. In this environment, the actions of all participants influence how others respond to the school program agendas. Learners enjoy sharing ideas, collaborating, cooperating, and helping other children. Therefore, school district leaders, principal, teachers, parents, and students should apply the following: school districts should give support by encouraging the multi-age school to carry out the school program action plan that targets the instructional core—improve multi-age curriculum, apply effective assessments, and apply appropriate instructional practices.

Principals support teachers by giving them suggestions and resources to be effective in their actions in the teaching and learning process. Teachers and teacher leaders support each other by collaborating, sharing ideas, and having conversations about quality educational practices. Parents need to stay involved in all activities of the school program, at home, and in the school building. And learners need to be cooperative and collaborate with all students and other members of the school community to make the school environment a friendly and trusting place for all.

APPLICATION OF CONCEPTS
FOR ALL SCHOOL SYSTEMS

All school programs should encourage the following:

- Schools should consider integrating the elements of a caring and trusting environment—respect for all, competence, integrity, and personal regard for others.
- Improve school culture by focusing on student learning, commit to high expectations for all students, support innovation, give time for reflective dialogue, and continue to search for different ways to approach the schooling organization.
- Create a shared school culture that allows teachers, teacher leaders, administration, parents, and students to collaborate ongoing and work together to make the school successful for all learners.

REFERENCES

Abplanalp, S. (2008). *Breaking the low-achieving mindset: A S.M.A.R.T. journey of purposeful change.* Madison, WI: QLD Learning (Quality Leadership by Design).

Bryk, A. S., & Schneider, B. (2003). Trust in schools: A core resource for school reform. *Educational Leadership, 60*(6), 40–45.

Burton, V. L. (2009). *Life story.* New York, NY: Houghton Mifflin Harcourt.

Comer, J. P., Haynes, N. M., Joyner, E. T., & Ben-Avie, M. (1996). *Rallying the whole village: The Comer process for reforming education.* New York, NY: Teachers College Press.

Deal, T. E., & Peterson, K. D. (2009). *Shaping school culture: Pitfalls, paradoxes, and promises.* San Francisco, CA: Jossey-Bass.

DuFour, R. (2007). Professional learning communities: A bandwagon, an idea worth considering, or our best hope for high levels of learning? *Middle School Journal, 39*(1), 4–8.

Geras, A. (2003). *Time for ballet.* New York, NY: Dial.

Hargreaves, A., & Fullan, M. (2012). *Professional capital: Transforming teaching in every school.* New York, NY: Teachers College Press.

Kochanek, J. R. (2005). *Building trust for better schools: Research-based practices.* Thousand Oaks, CA: Corwin Press.

Meier, D. (1995). *The power of their ideas: Lessons for America from a small school in Harlem.* Boston, MA: Beacon Press.

Schein, E. H. (2004). *Organizational culture and leadership* (3rd ed.). San Francisco, CA: Jossey-Bass.

Waters, J. T., Marzano, R. J., & McNulty, B. (2004). *Leadership that sparks learning. Educational Leadership, 61*(7), 48–51.

Wenger, E., McDermott, R., & Synder, W. (2002). *Cultivating communities of practice.* Boston, MA: Harvard Business School Press.

4

Building a Multi-Age School Culture—Elements to Consider

A teacher voices her opinion by saying, "Our students are just not performing well on tests and in class lessons. We are trying to follow the standards, but we find that the students cannot understand objectives. Is there another way to approach our classrooms to target the individual needs of the learners? Can we think about the multi-age approach?"

BUILDING A MULTI-AGE SCHOOL CULTURE

It is important to realize that to move from a single-grade to multi-age program is a process that does not need to be completed quickly. The transformation of the school environment into a multi-age program does not need to be immediate and total—it can happen over a few years and it can happen in only a few classrooms. The change-over should be planned based on what works best for the school environments.

Each school is very different. It is easier to gain the support of the school community and parents if the change is not abrupt. Parents and children may find gradual change more comfortable. Many teachers begin by teaming with other teachers on interdisciplinary units and sharing children from one grade with children in another grade for specific activities. The following guidelines will help schools think seriously about moving ahead with a multi-age environment:

- Each school is different, but share common reasons for deciding on a multi-age program. As mentioned in a previous chapter, there are two main reasons for making this transformation: to differentiate and offer an effective way to target individual needs of each learner with rigorous curricula; and, to assist with funding issues.

- Introducing the multi-age approach does not mean to start from the beginning. All programs build on what exists in the school already when considering expertise of staff and resources.
- Communication in the school community about multi-age learning environments is essential for gaining necessary support for the program. Leaders, teachers, parents, and students need to understand the change that is occurring and be part of the process so that they buy-in to the process.
- The entire school learning environment should share a common definition for the following: curriculum, environment, schedule and routine, assessment and evaluation, classroom management and multi-age learning settings. Even if all staff does not follow the multi-age philosophy, they still need to understand what it is and to be supportive of school efforts.

When making changes to the school program, all stakeholders need to be involved in the process. That means that central office administration, school leaders, teachers, staff, and parents must be made aware of the direction of the school and should be allowed to participate in the change process.

The entire school staff should have a common understanding of the multi-age philosophy and structure. This philosophy focuses on accommodating students' developmental needs by grouping students in a way so that students close in age may interact and collaborate with each other, on an ongoing basis. Children learn with children by modeling and observing others.

This philosophy should be integrated in the mission statement and the vision action plan of the school. To gain buy-in from all school community members, a committee should be organized to structure the planning phase. This committee should be open to all community members that want to be part of the change process. The next steps for the planning committee is to identify strengths of the school that are already in place that will support the program. The school members should review what is already happening that will support the program that they want to implement. It is a good idea to generate a list of what elements are important to their school environment and classrooms.

Complete change is not the issue in these schools because things that work well do not need to change. Some school elements from the traditional program should be integrated into the new multi-age program, if need be. For example, one school had a need for focusing on the environment because the school is in a suburban rural community that is influenced by nature. The school members are very interested in building an environmental center on the school campus. This is a good way that a school creates a school theme. In particular, this school community considered creating a school vision that focuses on environmental studies.

Different schools decide on different programs in their schools depending on background knowledge of the staff. Teachers might enjoy reading good informational text to kids. This encourages learners to gain content knowledge about a topic and the learners enjoy writing information pieces. Another teacher enjoys hands-on science experiments. This teacher always encourages learners to conduct observations, question hypotheses, and record and analyze data.

The point is that all teachers have specialty areas that they share with students to pique students' interests, as well as their own. School teams that are making the transition from graded to multi-age classrooms can generate a list of aspects of the school program that the school members plan to keep and things they would like to change. To do this, each school team should (a) obtain professional development on multi-age setting; (b) take courses or workshops; (c) visit other schools that are established multi-age programs; (d) read current educational articles and books; (e) reflect on the information and ideas that come from the multi-age resources and discuss what information is valuable to your own school program.

A school that is considering the change can initiate the process by trying out some components of the program: that is, integrate interdisciplinary planning and learning with other teachers and students; create workshop lessons and use fluid grouping to target skills for individual learners; set up orbital independent studies; conduct PLC meetings; or observe a lesson study.

Some schools move into the transition very slowly by meshing kindergarten with first grade the first year and building on the multi-age learning environment by adding a new multi-age classroom in the following year. Other schools feel that it is important to change the entire school all at once so that everyone in the school is following a multi-age learning environment model.

Some schools only select one or two grades to follow a multi-age program and do not integrate other classrooms in the model. Teachers and school members take ownership to this multi-age program when they share their expertise and engage in the creation of the program.

CURRICULUM DESIGN IN A MULTI-AGE CLASSROOM

Teachers need to consider the standards for writing multi-age curriculum. We try to rewrite these documents so that they are more helpful for teachers to plan and target necessary multi-age content understandings, concepts, and skills. The first step for teachers in planning curriculum is to consider at least three grade levels of standards so that students are targeted based on needs.

The question to consider during planning is, What do children really need to learn? When considering curriculum, students need to gain knowledge (content understandings, concepts, academic vocabulary, process skills, and skills in the discipline area). Teachers use three grade levels of standards to assist with targeting what learners need based on developmentally appropriate curriculum.

Social and emotional objectives should be considered when planning instruction. Some of the common elements in multi-age classes use the following: students direct their own learning so that they become independent learners and teachers conduct class meetings to discuss important expectations of the day.

Environment

An important aspect of organization in a multi-age learning environment is the classroom setting. Teachers should consider what they want to offer their students. Does the teacher want a quiet reading area where students may read and write in a quiet corner of the room? Does a teacher need a rug area where the class can all meet? Would a teacher like to include an area for the arts? Where are materials stored and where should students store their work and supplies?

Always have paper and pencils and art supplies in an area of the room so that learners may use these materials when needed for a task. Should the teacher use the outdoors for lessons? What are the traffic patterns in your classroom arrangement? It is wise to consider these issues and then draw a floor plan that fits your needs. This floor plan can be discussed with learners to gain their input. Also, continue to reflect on the drawing and room arrangement and do not hesitate to change things, if desired.

Communication

Communication is very important in a multi-age school program. Digital and paper newsletters should be sent out to the community at least once per month. The newsletter should discuss all the exciting learning experiences that have taken place and what future ideas are in the plans. Classroom events about curriculum, projects, themes, and internal and external events can be announced in a variety of formats.

It is always important that a school offer parent workshops that are offered by experts on multi-aging to assist parents on understanding how important this type of learning community can be for each child's learning progress. Also, a school should train parents and community volunteers to perform meaningful work in the multi-age classroom.

These volunteers can share expertise for enrichment tasks or just help in a group project. It is important to keep communication with all community members to keep them informed and involved in the program process. This will assist with the buy-in process of the multi-age program.

WHAT KINDS OF RESOURCES ARE NEEDED?

Multi-age programs need a variety of resources. These resources extend to reading materials, mathematics manipulatives, science equipment and materials, and art supplies. It is always suggested to send wish lists home to the parents so that they can help with supplies and materials. Also, rather than have the school purchase expensive textbooks for each subject area, it is wise to invest in a variety of levels of literature, information text, and poetry to help with the planning of targeting many learners' individual levels. Teacher resource books are important libraries to have in order to target a variety of lesson ideas.

WHAT QUESTIONS DO EDUCATOR
LEADERS AND TEACHERS HAVE?

The following information includes a list of some of the most common frequently asked questions that surface during professional development meetings on multi-age teaching and learning. The answers to these questions are kept brief so that any educator may consider the question and answer and apply the ideas in a specific school environment.

1. *How do we define multi-age teaching and learning?* The definition has important parts to consider. The multi-age philosophy in a school environment encourages teachers to target each student's strengths and needs while fitting the standard-based curriculum to the child, not the child to the curriculum. Differentiated instructional practices are embedded in the program. ELLs gain necessary content understandings in a very supportive environment that uses visuals and hands-on tasks. Also, student to student interaction assists ELLs to gain support when needed if the teacher is not able to give immediate support to the ELL.

   The structure of the multi-age program places students of varied ages together with the same teacher for two years. That means that the older children move on and a younger group of learners join the group that stays in the classroom. This type of structure is effective when considering how to target the needs of learners because the teacher and students know each other and do not need to get to know one another each year. Independent work during learning centers and orbital studies allows learners to target their interests and encourage students to become engaged in meaningful learning. Even though these strategies can be used in a graded system, the multi-age learning environment is student centered throughout all learning experiences. This allows the previously mentioned elements to become embedded in all activities of the multi-age learning environment.

2. *How does a multi-age learning environment look different from a graded classroom?* The multi-age classroom is a very active, authentic environment. Children interact with children on an ongoing basis. Because students support, collaborate, and become leaders, the atmosphere in the classroom is inviting and interesting. Students will feel at home in this situation. The rooms are showplaces that have authentic work samples that are child created and unique. Materials are organized around the learning environments that include many manipulatives, books, artifacts, and teacher/child-made items. The furniture allows for communication, collaboration and independent work. Word walls integrate academic vocabulary and bulletin boards are used for posting learning center management systems.

3. *What are the components of the program framework?* The program is rooted in shared leadership and team work. The components of the program are centered on 21st-century transformation of school culture: a transformational

leader, teacher leader, instructional rounds, lesson study, interdisciplinary teaching and learning, the workshop model, fluid grouping, problem-based learning and project-based lessons, differentiated instructional practices, learning centers, and orbital studies. These components are centered on a Common Core State Standards–based curriculum that is used to accommodate multi-age teaching and learning.

4. *How can a school implement a multi-age program?* The components mentioned earlier should be integrated into the program to assist a school to be successful. The process should be guided by an outside consultant so that professional development can be offered in an effective manner. It is suggested that a three-day professional development academy is offered so that all school members gain a clear understanding of the program components. An outreach program follows throughout the year to give instruction and support to community members, teachers, and administrators. This program should extend for three years.

5. *How do differentiated instructional practices connect to the multi-age program?* Differentiated practices are embedded into the multi-age program. Three characteristics of student learning processes guide the differentiated practices: readiness, interest, and learning profile (Tomlinson, 2001a) or multiple intelligences (MI) (Gardner, 1993). Readiness connects to the level that the learner is at based on their knowledgebase and skills of a topic. A teacher should create student interest by engaging the student in tasks that allow investigation and curiosity (Tomlinson, 2001a, 2001b). When considering the learner, the teacher should consider how a learner prefers to work on MI (linguistic, musical, logical-mathematical, spatial, kinesthetic, intrapersonal, interpersonal, naturalistic, and spiritualistic) and adapt learning for that student.

6. *Does the multi-age program address the learning processes of special needs learners and ELLs?* Special needs learners should be placed in the least restrictive instructional environments, preferably in regular education classrooms. ELLs need instructional approaches that connect to their learning styles. Some strategies for ELLs are using visuals, graphic organizers, and collaborative groups—scaffold approaches. The benefits to the diversity of students and students with special needs in the multi-age learning environment are: the program encourages the use of a variety of resources and alternative methods to target the needs of each learner. As an outcome to the program, all students are able to learn at pace that accommodates learners' needs.

7. *Do teachers always work in teams?* Teachers work in PLCs to plan and sometimes team teach units and lessons. The shared leadership environment encourages collaboration. "Teaming" has many definitions in the multi-age program. It can mean that teachers share ideas and materials or even share multi-age children during certain lesson tasks. It can also mean networking with other educators to share expertise and gain new insights into the teach-

ing and learning process. It can mean connecting with other teachers about successes and challenges. The teacher leader and other teachers continue to dialogue, participate in lesson study sessions and instructional rounds to assist with improvement of the multi-age program.

8. *Are multi-age classrooms teacher directed?* Teachers use a variety of teaching approaches such as the following: workshop teacher directed lessons, fluid grouping sessions, teacher as facilitator, and teacher as a supporter and provider of resources and materials.

9. *What are the advantages for the older students and the younger students in a multi-age classroom?* Older learners often become leaders in the classroom with younger students because they have been in the classroom for a longer time and usually have a stronger knowledgebase in certain areas of the curriculum. Younger students tend to learn from the older children through observations and modelling.

10. *What about assessment and report cards in a multi-age program?* Assessment has three different levels: formative (daily assessment tasks), common formative assessments (assessments that are conducted across the school community), and benchmarks and summative assessments (tests given at different parts of the school year). Report cards are based on standards that must be met. The report system identifies different levels of goals at each level of the marking period and the reporting process addresses how the goals have or have not been reached by each student (see figure 4.1). The variety of levels of assessment gives an appropriate profile of how the student is progressing in all areas of the curriculum.

11. *How do we launch a multi-age program?* Launching the MAC program in any school system means that administrators, teachers, and staff need to take the time to prepare. Culture in a school system is important because it takes an enormous amount of learning for everyone in the system. First, the school community needs to consider how to transform the school culture into a shared community of learners. It is advisable that educators learn how, as a group, to tackle new skills and acquire new knowledge in the implementation of the multi-age learning setting. The school system should consider just how to give support to a safe and trusting school environment for students and organizational learning.

12. *Who should be involved?* District leaders need to convene principals to encourage them to become part of the multi-age network in the district. The district leaders can gain their support by discussing just how the schools will receive professional development and resources. Once the district gains support by a school principal, then the district should send in the consultants that will provide the professional development program. In the case where teachers talk to teachers and make decisions on how to move ahead with a multi-age program, it is the teachers that encourage school administrators and district members to support their innovative ideas. Each circumstance is different,

Social and Emotional Skills   JAN   JUNE

	JAN	JUNE
Knows his/her full (first and last) name		
Respects and shows concern for people and things around him/her		
Plays and works on projects and shares cooperatively with other children		
Has made friends at school and gets along with others		
Participates in group activities		
Focuses on tasks		

Work Habits

Follows routines independently		
Follows basic directions – in centers, PBL and Orbital studies		
Can work in small groups/ collaborate with others		
Is learning to respect others while they work – takes on leadership roles		
Participates in clean-up		

Listening / Speaking Skills

Plays with words, sounds and rhymes		
Shares ideas through Readers Theater tasks		
Shares information for group work		
Answers questions with appropriate information		
Asks questions to gain knowledge		
Responds to comments & questions from others		

Fine Motor Skills

Print and cursive writing is appropriate for age		
Can complete puzzles appropriate for age		

Social Studies/Science (add as needed)

Environmental Studies Unit – projects completed		
Field based observations, collection of data, use of data		

Language Arts / Literacy

	JAN	JUNE
To comprehend range of literary genres		
To connect reading and writing in tasks		
To become competent in decoding and encoding information		
Reads independently age appropriate text		
Makes reading and writing lifelong tasks to gain information with independent projects		
Writings as an Author – follows process, confers, shares, edits, publishes		
Writes in content areas – journals, projects, independent work		

Mathematics

Literate in mathematical understandings in all content strands		
Read math situations/problems and understand them		
Skilled in using math computations		
Use math thinking to problem solve		
Use math journal to express math ideas and solutions		

Interdisciplinary Learning

Brainstorms ideas for theme/unit of study		
Shares appropriate ideas on the topic		
Participates in learning tasks for topic		
Completes projects associated with topic		

MARKING CODE

G - Good Progress
W - Working on skill, needs time to develop
NM - Not measured at this time

Attendance	Jan.	June
Days Absent		
Days Late		

COMMENTS:

Conference Requested: Teacher _____ Parent _____

Parent Signature _____

Lower School Progress Report
Multi-age Communities

Name _____

School _____

Teacher _____

Principal _____

Figure 4.1.   Report Card—Lower School

and educators will need to figure out what works best in the school situation. A key consideration is what resources are available, how to get buy-in from staff, and how will you introduce the program to the school community.

13. *How fast do schools move from a traditional program to a multi-age learning environment?* Every school is different. Some schools move very slowly, changing two grades per year into a multi-age school environment. Some schools restructure all grades and other schools only change two grades into multi-age programs. Some schools only multi-age during certain times during the day or week. All strategies work based on the needs of the school programs.

14. *Why should a school system select to transform schools into multi-age classrooms?* We know that we need effective strategies to help all students learn on high levels to have the skills for the 21st century that are focused on problem solving, communication, collaboration, high-level thinking, leadership qualities, and technological advances. The multi-age program allows students to develop these skills in an active learning environment that encourages these skills and lifelong independent learning skills.

15. *How does this multi-age program connect to grade level high stakes testing processes?* Students continue to take benchmark tests or high stakes tests based on grade levels. The multi-age students are learning based on Common Core State Standards and students are assessed on how well they are meeting grade-level standards as well as standards that are a year below and a year above the student's grade level. Students do very well on high-stakes tests because the MAC program allows students to work at their own level. Teachers continue to evaluate each student's performance to make sure each student meets the current grade level needs.

16. *What kind of commitment and understanding should the MAC group have?* The MAC program encourages multi-age learning to target individual needs of each student. Each school environment is unique but will share some common elements. The MAC program described in this book represents possibilities on how educators can transform the school for the 21st century in a very positive way. Teachers and administrators decide on what elements fit their school and community. As mentioned in this book, introducing a multi-age approach does not mean starting from scratch. A school should build on past experience and the expertise that already exists in the school building.

17. *How does one get buy-in?* To get buy-in, teachers and administrators collaborate on a mission statement and action plan. These documents allow all school members to give input on creating a common understanding of a multi-age program in their school. Even if all staff members do not entirely agree with the endeavor, they do need to understand the philosophy and what it is that is being accomplished. The staff will show support, whenever possible.

18. *Do all teachers work in teams in a multi-age program?* Teachers have numerous opportunities to work together with other colleagues. Teachers plan curriculum units and discuss students' progress during multi-age professional learning

communities. Teachers do not feel isolated because they do not shut the door and work alone. These teachers are professionals making collaborative educational decisions to target students' needs. The important issue is that teachers and administrators in a school take it step by step, gradually and comfortably. The school teachers, administrators, parents, and members of the community working on this endeavor give strong support for the program.

19. *What kinds of resources are needed?* The multi-age program needs a variety of materials for hands-on mathematics and science tasks and numerous reading materials on many different levels to target the needs of multi-age learners.

20. *How are report cards used in a multi-age program?* The report card should be standards based and target the subject area concepts. Reports cards tend to use a rating scale from 1–5 and integrate narratives that allow the teacher to write anecdotal notes to the parents about what, why, and how their child does things. It is important to set goals as part as the reporting process with students and parents at the beginning of each marking period. The reporting process addresses how the goals have or have not been reached.

SNAPSHOT OF A NEW MULTI-AGE SCHOOL PROCESS

A district meeting was called into session with all district leaders. An outside consultant presented a PowerPoint that addressed Multi-Age School Programs. The components included: target individual needs of the learner, encourage high-level thinking, collaboration, problem-based lessons, and independent learning. The presenter discussed how these components connect to current 21st-century trends in education. The superintendent asks each school leader to consider the school reform agenda.

Following this meeting, a presentation to school environments took place at each school site. Teachers had questions such as: How can we make the change from the traditional program? Will we receive professional development ongoing and the support from the district? Will parents be informed of the school reform agenda? How will buy in to the program take place? The district and school building principals assured the teachers that they would not be asked to make these changes alone. Support and resources will be given where needed and professional development will be an ongoing process. Teachers feel uneasy, but agree to participate in the re-culture of the school environment.

EDUCATOR'S REFLECTION

This chapter answers many of the foundation questions that school districts and schools have in regard to the multi-age program. It is important to realize that each school is different, but share common reasons for deciding on transforming schools to a multi-age program. This program helps to embed differentiation. It encourages independent learning, high-level thinking, and problem-based learning.

All staff and parents take part in the process for setting up the program, so that all school members have buy-in to the learning environment. The school district and school must support the program by providing appropriate professional development that is ongoing and give support and resources needed to implement the multi-age agenda.

Most importantly, the entire school learning environment should develop and share a common definition for defining the multi-age program: multi-age curriculum, schedule, routines, assessment, and class management systems. All members of the school need to understand the multi-age philosophy and support the school efforts.

APPLICATION OF CONCEPTS FOR ALL SCHOOL SYSTEMS

All school programs should encourage the following:

- Students should be given a rigorous program that encourages high-level thinking and independent learning.
- Curriculum should target individual needs of all learners.
- School reform can change schools for the betterment of all students.
- Each school should reflect on just how effective change can be made in the school program.

REFERENCES

Gardner, H. (1993). *Multiple intelligences: The theory in practice.* New York, NY: Basic Books.

Tomlinson, C. A. (2001a). *Differentiation of instruction in the elementary grades.* Champaign, IL: ERIC Clearinghouse on Elementary and Early Childhood Education. (ERIC Document No. ED443572)

Tomlinson, C. A. (2001b). *How to differentiate instruction in mixed ability classrooms* (2nd ed.). Alexandria, VA: Association for Supervision and Curriculum Development.

III

THE LEARNING PROCESS

5

Instructional Components for a Multi-Age Program

After interviewing teachers that are making the switch from traditional to multi-age classrooms, many questions surfaced. Some common questions:

- *"I am confused and nervous about planning lessons with mixed age students in a classroom."*
- *"The multi-age classrooms look active and exciting, but I just do not think I can manage a class like that."*
- *"What do I do when I need to teach reading skills?"*
- *"How do I make sure that all students understand the mathematics that they need to know?"*
- *"How do I organize lessons to target the needs of all students with mixed ages?"*
- *"How do I manage my classroom to accommodate all students in this environment?"*
- *"How do I know what my classroom should look like in terms of physical space?"*

Most multi-age teachers are confused and nervous about planning lessons with mixed ages in a classroom. These teachers have thought about trying to implement reading workshop, math workshop, and other subject areas. But, teachers all have one common statement: "I am not quite sure how to accomplish this multi-age instructional plan." This uneasiness expressed about teaching more than one grade level in a classroom, carries over in all subjects, not just in literacy and mathematics.

The following section targets the issue of how to create a learning environment that addresses the needs of every student in a multi-age classroom. The learning process, discussed in chapters 5, 6, and 7, integrate an instructional framework and curriculum ideas that are workable and adaptable for any multi-age class.

Teacher Directed (Workshop Model) Lesson
- Pre-information
- Teach Concept
- Independent Group Work
- Individual reflective writing
- Share/Debrief Whole Class

Fluid Grouping (Partners, Small Groups)
- Teacher forms small groups to target the needs of learners based on the whole class lesson objectives
- Guided small-group support or strategy lessons
- Based on Concepts, Skills, and Processes
- Groups working independently on skills and objectives while one group is guided by teacher

Problem-Based Learning (During Interdisciplinary Studies)
- Connect topic of study to real world problems
- Support rigorous curriculum, inquiry, authentic learning
- Independent group work
- Problem or question to investigate

Independent Learning
- Investigate a topic of interest
- Independent individual or group work
- Teacher support

Learning Centers
- Focus on topics of study
- Teach, reinforce, or enrich concepts
- Individual, partner, or group work
- Variety of materials and resources
- Assess, recordkeeping, monitor

*scaffolding and differentiated instructional practice (embedded in all tasks)

Figure 5.1.   MAC Instructional Components
Source: Adapted from Siena (2009).

Chapter 5 initiates discussion on how to define the range of instructional components for implementing lessons in a multi-age classroom: direct instruction lesson (workshop style), fluid grouping, scaffolding, differentiated teaching and learning, project-based instruction, independent learning, and learning centers. The range of multi-age instructional components is defined in figure 5.1.

This chapter also describes what a physical learning environment looks like in order to meet the needs of this multi-age program and what a teacher should know and do when managing this type of classroom. The range of lesson components is addressed in detail, in the order they are listed on the framework.

TEACHER DIRECTED (WORKSHOP MODEL) MINI LESSON IN A MULTI-AGE CLASSROOM

It is important to note that the very first question of a teacher or administrator placed in multi-age learning community classrooms is the following: How do I teach to a multi-age group? The multi-age classroom instructional practices call for a very specific framework that allows for addressing all learners' needs. It is important to emphasize that the teacher in this type of classroom does not teach with a cross-grade approach—an approach that allows the teacher to separate students of each grade into grade work groups to target grade-level instruction.

The multi-age classroom targets multi-age students considering the developmental appropriate level that each child is at. This process involves teachers meeting children where they are, both as individuals and as part of a group, and helping each student meet challenging and achievable learning goals (NAEYC, 2009). This program creates the school community around the learner's needs.

It was mentioned in chapter 1 that Goodlad and Anderson (1987) believed that a multi-age learning setting is appropriate, rather than the graded system, for reason that students are given the freedom to develop at a pace that is optimal for his/her needs. Teachers have found this model effective in a number of subjects. This multi-age lesson structure supports independence, understanding, rigor, and differentiation in all subject areas.

Currently, teachers often feel bombarded by a stream of mandates, new approaches, and curricula. While educators may be a bit wary of the next big approach to learning (such as multi-age), the next big issue is always worth investigating—will this approach help to improve students' learning?

The first step in the multi-age instructional framework is the teacher-directed workshop model. The workshop model developed for literacy is a mini-lesson strategy used across the curriculum (Siena, 2009). The multi-age teacher finds that a mini lesson of 10–15 minutes provides the whole multi-age class direct and explicit instruction in one of the following ways: teach a key concept, direct students in a problem-solving task, read and think aloud for a specific purpose, demonstrate a writing process strategy, or model just how the expectation of a project might look like.

Although the times may vary, the instructional components define the routines for seamless multi-age whole group classroom instruction. The pre-lesson introduction component that should take no more than 5 minutes (a component added to the workshop model), facilitates the tone for learning by setting lesson expectations. The teacher posts the learning expectations and Common Core State Standards (for at least three grade levels), on a chart paper or a Smart Board, and proceeds to read and review the information with the learners. This agenda includes the work to be done, the content and concepts to learn in the mini lesson and the expectations for the completed task of the lesson.

Calkins (2001) emphasized that we should not ask low-level questions to begin a mini lesson such as "Who remembers what we did yesterday?" or "Who knows what a fraction means?" A successful mini lesson should always begin by connecting the day's work to the larger context of the unit—what students did the previous day or what they are about to do.

For example, Anna, a Voyager teacher (grades 4 and 5), says to her students during a science lesson, "Yesterday I noticed that some of you were classifying a 'solid' as a big rock. Today we are going to investigate different ways to think of solids, liquids, and gases. We are going to find examples of solids, liquids, and gases found in the local environment."

The mini lesson follows with the teacher providing the content of the lesson. In literacy, this means teaching a strategy or skill that is useful to the multi-age learners. In mathematics, the lesson may include a mathematics concept or include defining mathematics vocabulary. A mini lesson follows these specific steps: pre-information, teach concept or skill, independent group work, reflective writing and a debriefing session.

The teaching phase of the lesson may also include asking a student to model a strategy from the lesson while others observe. Whatever the subject, a mini-lesson should be no longer than 10–15 minutes. Let us look at how the workshop model works in a multi-age 3–4 literacy class.

SNAPSHOT OF A WORKSHOP MODEL LESSON

Mary Alice, a Detective teacher (grades 3 and 4), decides that after many observations of her students, she has found that her readers are used to answering questions, but not asking them as they read. She feels that questioning is a critical comprehension strategy that helps readers construct and extend meaning (Richardson, 2009). Mary Alice decides to conduct a mini lesson around question cards, a task adapted from QAR strategy (Raphael, 1982).

The teacher starts the lesson by reading the expectations of the lesson from the chart paper: "We will work with a partner today and read a story together. Partners will take turns for five minutes and read two pages. I am distributing a green, yellow, and red question card to each group. Begin with green questions and gradually work toward yellow and red questions. The green card questions are found in one place in the text. Go directly to the text and find the answer to the questions: Who? What? Where? When? How?

"If you can find the answers to the green card questions you and your partner should move to the yellow questions. You must slow down and look in more than one place in the text to answer the following kinds of yellow questions: Compare: How are ____ and ____ similar? Contrast: How are ____ and ____ different? Main idea/details: What are some examples of the main idea? Give some details to support the main idea. If you are able to move to the red questions you and your partner should stop and think about the passage and what you know in order to answer the following: I wonder why . . . Why do you think . . . ? What would have happened if . . . ? Partners may use small sticky notes to mark the important areas of the passage to help with answers to the questions. Partners have today and tomorrow to complete the lesson tasks. I will move around to partners to see how you are doing."

Before we break, let us model two green questions using the book *The Mouse and the Motorcycle* by Beverly Cleary (2006). The teacher asks Dylan to find evidence in the story that answers the questions "Who is the character?" (Ralph) "And, what does Ralph want to do?" (Ralph wants to venture outside.) The teacher asks the student to find the clues in the story and place sticky notes to hold the place that answers the two questions. Then, the learner reads to the whole class the evidence from the story that answers the questions.

An important aspect of this mini lesson is that the teacher asked a student to try out the strategy while the rest of the class observed. Students are more likely to be successful independently if they observe or try the strategy in the whole group before working on their own.

A brief mini lesson is an effective tool because the need for independent work is great. Once the mini lesson is finished, students are asked to work independently, in small groups, or pairs (as in the lesson example shown earlier). Students are heterogeneously grouped in multi-ages and levels of ability. The teacher's role is to circulate for 5 minutes to ensure all students are on task, confer with group members to give individual instruction, ask questions, observe, and take anecdotal notes.

The purpose of this type of grouping in a lesson is to allow all multi-age students to learn from each other, share expertise, and change points of view. Learners are asked to collaborate, cooperate, take leadership roles, gain new knowledge based on individual needs, and take responsibility for their own learning. What this means is that scaffolding and differentiation are embedded in this process. While the term "workshop model" means different things to different teachers, what is consistent is that the multi-age workshop model for any subject area, always integrates instruction, practice (independently alone, with pairs or in small groups), and reflection.

The next phase (that has been added to the multi-age workshop model) is the *writing and reflecting phase* for the learner. Each learner reflects on the learning process of the lesson in a personal journal answering the generic questions: What did I learn in this lesson that is new? What did I find interesting? What challenges did I have? How does this lesson connect to my learning in other subjects? What did I need to know before this lesson? Did I enjoy this lesson? Why? Why not?

This writing task is an excellent tool for assessing what a learner knows and does not know from the lesson. Of cause, the questions should be revised according to the age of the learners. What is important is that teachers can review journals ongoing. More information on how this writing tool is implemented in the multi-age class as a formative assessment strategy is discussed in chapter 7.

The last phase of this workshop style lesson is to debrief or conduct share time with the whole multi-age class. Each group recaps the steps followed and reviews solutions to the lesson tasks. For example, partners share answers to the green, yellow, and red cards. Sometimes at this stage a student is asked to share a partner's thinking. This move supports a partner whose original idea was not as strong as the other partner, but who got a lot out of listening. Listening is an important skill that should be developed in all lessons (Siena, 2009). Discussion always ends with a prompt by the teacher to ask which group presentations were reasonable answers.

A multi-age workshop model generally lasts 60–90 minutes. The teacher and students have specific roles in the workshop model. To recap, the multi-age workshop model contains the components shown in table 5.1.

The next step in the multi-age lesson framework suggests that a teacher follow up the workshop model lesson with fluid grouping.

FLUID GROUPING

Fluid grouping (sometimes labeled flexible grouping) in a multi-age learning community is defined as a small group teaching model that looks at a learner's needs and addresses those needs during a small group instructional process. The assessment process in the workshop lesson provides information to determine the level of each student for determining fluid grouping objectives. Once the teacher reviews what each student knows or does not know in the workshop lesson, then fluid groups are organized.

Some groups will address re-teaching of the concept, while other groups will address more challenging work. The fluid group model integrates the following factors: look at student's needs and continue to assess each learner to determine the level of the student based on content, concepts, and skills. It is important for the teacher to use formative assessments in this process. The teacher continues to make changes to the fluid group when a student masters skills or needs more help. Evaluation should take place often in this process to allow students to move ahead in the learning process.

Table 5.1. Components of a Multi-Age Lesson Workshop Model

Components and Stages	Teacher Role	Student Role
Pre-Lesson Stage (5 minutes)	Post lesson expectations, standards, and lesson targets on chart paper or Smart Board. Facilitates tone of lesson by setting lesson expectations.	Understands what to do before lesson— assignment, content and concepts for understanding.
Mini-Lesson Stage (10–15 minutes)	Multi-age whole class direct and explicit instruction: • teach concept • direct a problem solving task • read and think aloud for purpose • demonstrate a writing strategy • model expectations of a project	Understand the learning targets.
Independent Work Stage (30 minutes)	Circulate for 5 minutes to ensure all students are on task. Confer with group members to give individual instruction. Ask questions. Observe and take anecdotal notes.	Learn from each other, share expertise, change viewpoints, collaborate, cooperate, take leadership roles, gain new knowledge, take responsibility of learning.
Writing and Reflecting Stage (10 minutes)	Allow students to write and reflect in personal journals with generic questions. Teacher reviews each journal as an assessment tool.	Students reflect in personal journal: What did I learn? What did I find interesting? What challenges did I have? How does this lesson connect to my learning in other subjects? What did I need to know before this lesson? Did I enjoy the lesson?
Debrief/Share Stage (5 minutes)	Discussion prompted by teacher.	Each multi-age student group recaps steps and solutions and discusses best answer from the whole group discussion.

Fluid grouping is not individualized instruction, not a chaotic unstructured process, not another way to homogenously group multi-age students, and certainly not a one-size-fits-all approach to teaching and learning. It is a strategy to teach concepts to learners based on the needs of students that derive from the workshop lesson.

For example, a young learner in the Explorer class (kindergarten and grade 1) who can decode words with short vowel sounds in a direct instruction workshop lesson would be placed the following day, in a fluid group that focuses on a new phonics skill. Since this student already knows short vowel sounds he or she advances to learn new concepts. In the Voyager class (grades 4–5) mathematics lesson on subtraction, a core group of students benefit by learning more about renaming two-digit numbers during the subtraction process. One group needs reteaching on the regrouping concepts with two-digit numbers and another group needs a more advanced instruction lesson on using three-digit numbers and renaming in subtraction.

Fluid grouping maximizes student growth and ensures the needs of an individual student are met. Teachers realize that a student is not always ready to accept what teachers have to offer in a lesson. Learners in a multi-age program have the opportunity to retake, redo, or rethink what they are asked to learn. It is the teacher's responsibility to offer numerous opportunities for a learner to experience the same concepts in different tasks or move the learner to a new concept when the learner is ready.

During the 15 minutes that teachers focus attention on a small fluid group, the rest of the students work independently on their own situations based on their needs. Students learn that, during such fluid group lessons, the teacher is available in time. They are taught that they need to seek out other students for finding answers to any questions that surface during this independent time.

We have found that fluid grouping in a multi-age classroom allows the teacher to teach to the needs of each learner and this type of opportunity for students and working arrangements is a positive component for a multi-age learning community.

PROJECT-BASED LEARNING INSTRUCTION

PBL is an instructional strategy that engages students in the learning of content, concepts, and process skills. PBL allows learners to use an exciting and innovative format to connect topics of study to real-world problems and the community (Bender, 2012). This strategy is supported by many educators (Barell, 2010; Cole & Washburn-Moses, 2010) because it encourages a rigorous curriculum and an inquiry-based course of study applied to an authentic learning task.

PBL in the multi-age learning environment is defined as a highly motivated assignment that connects to an engaging question, task, or problem. Small groups in this program select their group project based on the topic and content that is connected to their interdisciplinary workshop theme that meets at least twice per week and are team taught by more than one teacher. See chapter 7 for an understanding of how the PBL process is scheduled, designed, and implemented in the multi-age learning community.

Multi-age students collaborate on a project and work cooperatively to solve a question or problem that is presented by the teacher (Barell, 2010; Grant, 2010). Then, learners investigate appropriate information, define the problem, locate and use valid resources, make decisions about how to find solutions, select a product that fits the solution to the problem and then share the solution and the product's effectiveness (Tomlinson, 2005, 2014) to the whole class.

Some ideas found in a PBL interdisciplinary multi-age theme workshop are the following:

SNAPSHOT OF PROJECT-BASED LEARNING

Two teachers of the Hippopotamus class (grades 2–3) and Eagles class (grades 4–5) team teach an interdisciplinary workshop on what constitutes a healthy diet. The PBL problem given to small multi-age groups is "What is a healthy diet?" Students participate in interdisciplinary workshops for two weeks learning about nutrition through science food experiments, research on the Internet about the human body and nutrition, and read and write informational text on the topic.

Groups are asked to interview the school nutritionist, visit food markets, and collect and analyze data on their daily intake of food. As a culminating PBL project, students use the data collected in each group plan and conduct an awareness-raising campaign about nutrition in their local school and community by creating digital posters and flyers. These projects are presented to parents and community members at an evening open house at the school.

This PBL assignment process takes as long as the interdisciplinary theme is studied. The process block can vary from two to six weeks. This type of assignment allows multi-age students to use varied learning strengths, share expertise, change perspectives, work independently with others, and allow learners to gain new knowledge of a theme based on prior understandings.

INDEPENDENT LEARNING

Independent learning is a process through which a student and teacher identify topics of interest. In this multi-age program this independent work is an event separate from daily lessons, interdisciplinary studies, and PBL assignments. Both student and teacher participate in this method of investigating a problem or topic and identifying how to go about the studies.

Independent work can be with an individual student, pairs, or groups of students. It depends on the objective of the independent task. This strategy is an excellent way to build on student interest and allows the student maximum freedom to work

(Tomlinson, 2014). The teacher provides ongoing support to ensure high standards of production, and students use process logs to document the process the student follows throughout the independent learning process.

One example of an independent learning task is a Marshall class (grades 6–8 learners) selecting a book to read based on interest. The teacher conferences with each learner (once per week), and is scheduled to find out what the student is gaining from this experience. The process log is reviewed and the teacher gives input of the next steps that the student should follow during this independent learning experience.

Another example is a learner from the Elephant class (K–1) wants to investigate the moon in the sky. The young learner creates a moon book and draws what she observes in the sky each day. The process log is a shape book of the moon phases. The teacher conferences with the learner to suggest an informational text she may read to gain more of an understanding of the moon's changing phases.

LEARNING CENTERS

A learning center in a multi-age learning environment is often a classroom area that contains a collection of tasks with appropriate materials designed to teach, reinforce, or extend a particular skill or concept (Kaplan, Kaplan, Madsen, & Gould, 1980). Learning Centers are separate tasks used to explore topics or practice skills.

Teachers adjust learning centers for the readiness levels of students based on reteaching, instructional, and enriching levels of concepts of topics that are studied in the classroom. The teacher matches with learner's skill level; encourages continuous development of learner; and, allows opportunity to match task with students' learning styles.

Some issues to consider: avoid having all learners do all work at all centers; teach students to manage materials and record their own progress at centers; have clear directions and criteria for success at each center, and monitor what students accomplish (Tomlinson, 2014).

Multi-age teachers should consider:

- Focusing on topics of study or interest.
- Integrating learning targets with standards.
- Using a variety of materials that encourage growth in learning for all learners.
- Integrating tasks that are designed from simple to complex, structured and open-ended, concrete, semi-concrete, and abstract.
- Preparing instructions for a learner to manage the center tasks.
- Reminding students what to do if they need help.
- Providing an assessment system and record-keeping chart to monitor events.

Learning center tasks are often teacher made and focus on mastery or extension of concept, skills, and processes based on unit of study and lessons. This center time is a way that multi-age classrooms collaborate on tasks.

For example, teachers from the Elephant class (K–1) and Hippopotamus class (grades 2–3) decided to create mathematics learning centers for both classes. The Multi-Age Classroom Center was set up in a corner of the hallway outside their classrooms. Since both classrooms were studying geometry in mathematics workshop, the teachers decided to set up learning center tasks that would target different levels of understanding for geometrical concepts. The teachers decided to take the tasks from Marilyn Burns, *About Teaching Mathematics: A K–8 Resource* (2007). The tasks were as follows:

- **Task 1:** Sorting shapes on the geoboard. Each student is asked to make a shape using one rubber band. Then, the student draws the shape on dot paper and sorts the shape on the center bulletin board with other shapes.
- **Task 2:** Square up. This center game is for two players. Each player takes twelve cubes in one color. The partners take turns putting one cube of the color on an empty peg on the geoboard. When the learner thinks four of the cubes mark the corners of a square, he or she says "Square up." Then the other partner says, "Prove it." Prove it by stretching a rubber band around the pegs the partner has marked.
- **Task 3:** Geoboard Line Segments. Each learner finds the next-to-the-longest line segment he or she can make on the geoboard. The child must write down on the center recording poster, why he or she is sure the answer is correct.
- **Task 4:** Areas of Four on the Geoboard. The Square made by stretching a rubber band around four pegs with no pegs inside has an area of 1 square unit. The learner must find other shapes with an area of four square units. The learner records the shapes on small geoboard dot paper. The learner chooses one shape, copies it on large geoboard dot paper, cuts it out, and posts it on the center board. The learner must post only a shape that is different from those already posted.

These learning centers are at different levels of learning and students may complete tasks that they are able to do. This strategy is a way to have students redo, learn, and enrich their understandings about topics.

SCAFFOLDING IN A MULTI-AGE CLASSROOM

Scaffolding in a multi-age classroom is described as a strategy to support learning. The support for the learner comes from the teacher or other multi-age classmates. The teacher or another student helps the learner master a task or concept that the learner is unable to grasp independently. It is important to allow the learner to work through the task as much as possible without assistance. The teacher or other students help the learner with problems that are too difficult for the learner to understand.

It is also important to allow the learner to make mistakes. The teacher or classmates gauge feedback to the learner based on his or her mistakes. Through this process the learner is able to accomplish the task. Once the learner can do the task independently, the teacher or other classmates fade away from this learner (gradually removing the scaffolding).

In a multi-age classroom, this scaffolding approach is used frequently because students learn from other students in a natural way through the interactive learning community atmosphere. Many interactive tasks can be observed during multi-age learning such as: thinking aloud between student to student, cooperative group discussions, modeling from teacher or older student to younger student, having conversations with peers during independent work, giving tips to friends, or just breaking the task into smaller, more manageable parts.

It is important that the teacher observe the scaffolding interactions that are going on in the learning environment for reason that tasks or skills too difficult or too simple for the learner can only cause frustration for the student. The teacher should have a clear understanding of the learner's prior knowledge and abilities. This information can be gained through having ongoing conversations with a learner to redirect any misconceptions and to target the learner's individual needs.

DIFFERENTIATION IN THE MULTI-AGE CLASSROOM

Differentiation in a multi-age classroom is embedded in the program. Tomlinson and Imbeau (2010) stated that "the purpose of a differentiated classroom is to make sure that there is opportunity and support for each student to learn essential knowledge and skills as effectively and efficiently as possible. In other words, differentiation occurs to 'make room' for all kinds of learners to succeed academically."

This process is not a single strategy but rather an instructional approach that integrates a variety of strategies during teaching and learning. Differentiation allows all students in the multi-age learning environment to access the same classroom curriculum by providing learning tasks that are tailored to students' needs (Hall, Strangman, & Meyer, 2003).

The multi-age teacher incorporates differentiated strategies based on the assessed needs of their students. It is imperative that throughout a unit of study, teachers assess students informally by taking anecdotal notes, examining student products, and asking student questions. The assessments help to determine what level a learner is at and this information will allow a teacher to adapt the assignments to the developmental needs of the multi-age learner. Individualized instruction is applied as needed.

For example, in the multi-age learning community a teacher or a learner works one-on-one with a confused student, a teacher or student stands next to a learner to refocus him or her, or suggest that a student turn the lined paper sideways to create columns for vocabulary work. Because all students are teachers, this type of individualized attention occurs ongoing throughout the learning process.

A multi-age learning environment might include tiered assignments designed to target the same content and objectives, but the process or product is varied according to the learner's level of readiness. During a 2–3 reading lesson, learners with moderate comprehension skills are asked to create a story-web. Learners with advanced comprehension skills are asked to retell a story from the point of view of the main character.

PHYSICAL ENVIRONMENT

The physical environment of a multi-age classroom should be flexible in nature because learners of different ages continue to group and regroup in this learning community. It is important to keep a particular seating area for learners that they can always begin at and return to after moving around the room for specific learning tasks. This seating area can have a specific seat for each learner or hold a space at a table of a group of learners. This type of seating helps with attendance, dismissal, and assists the teacher to create order quickly at the end of a learning experience. The flexibility occurs because many times each learner is called to other parts of the room or other parts of the school building to participate in learning tasks (Richardson, 2009). It is so important that the teacher keep the room flexible, flexible, and flexible! Some elements to consider integrating in the physical space:

- Have a meeting area where all students can fit comfortably to have discussions during the day.
- Have a library with numerous level books and writing materials. A rug often defines the area for quiet reading time.
- Try to have a shelf area where mathematics, social studies, and science materials are stored.
- Display learners' work ongoing around the room to decorate the learning environment.
- Post chart paper around the classroom to remind students of current topics, concepts, and procedures that are currently discussed and include procedural posters for math problem solving, reading, and writing processes and common rules to follow.

The important rule is to keep the classroom colorful, inviting, and attractive that includes students' work samples, projects, and ideas.

MANAGING A MULTI-AGE CLASSROOM

The skilled multi-age teacher organizes and focuses curriculum on essential information, understandings, and skills based on the Common Core State Standards. The teachers in the program use three to four grade levels to guide curriculum instruction. For example, a teacher in a 4–5 classroom considers standards for grades 3, 4, 5, and 6. This is done so that the curriculum is designed to meet the developmental levels of all learners in the program. Chapter 6 will discuss more planning processes for the design of multi-age curriculum.

The multi-age teacher uses time in a flexible manner. Sometimes a fluid lesson will need to meet for over 1 hour during the day because students need extra guidance with understanding concepts. This flexibility in the schedule does not impede the daily learning process of learners. Sometimes the teacher needs time to diagnose student needs and craft learning experiences in response to the diagnoses.

The teacher's job is to anticipate potential issues that may arise in the schedule and structure student work to avoid those possible problems. A good solution is to have students become involved with independent projects. If time permits, students may work on such tasks to overcome scheduling issues.

Teachers should always consider that he or she shares responsibility for teaching and learning with all multi-age students. There are many teachers in this learning community and learners must realize that they all need to take on leadership roles from time to time. Teachers and students are collaborators in learning. Time, materials, modes of instruction, ways of grouping, ways of expressing and assessing learning, and other class elements are tools that can be used in the management of the multi-age classroom to promote individual and whole class success.

Time is a very important issue in a multi-age learning environment. Some solutions are the following:

- Analyze your day schedule and set priorities.
- Eliminate tasks that have little education value (such as worksheets or free time for students). Make every minute count.
- Teach all students to manage their own classroom by making the children accountable for putting materials in their proper place, handing out lesson resources, keeping the reading or math corner tidy, and cleaning up after workstation and independent activities.
- Learners should conduct morning routines (counting lunch, taking attendance) with the teacher's input. Practice of these tasks will teach students each task that is needed. Learners should not waste time trying to find materials or cleaning up the space because the last team or group did not follow procedures for cleanup.
- Always manage transitions from one lesson task to another. Many students are grouped and regrouped ongoing in a multi-age classroom. The teacher should practice transitions until students can rotate between tasks in less than one or two minutes. And, use a timer for lessons and activities. It is easy to unintentionally extend a whole group lesson or fluid group session beyond the schedule time.
- Since multi-age learners are moving around in an active learning environment, reasonable limits during independent work need to be discussed. First, teach

all students to use a whisper voice. A teacher can have a whisper monitor that allows students to use a whisper voice. The teacher should also use a soft voice during meeting with small groups. A bell, a clap pattern, music, or rhyme should be used to demand the attention of the whole multi-age group.

Teachers organize their classrooms so that they are not interrupted during fluid grouping sessions. To avoid problems, the teacher models and learners practice routines so multi-age students know exactly what to do during group work, learning centers, or just completing independent projects. If students do interrupt often, analyze the work assigned. Is the work too complex for the learner? Students need to be successful during independent time. Also, teach learners that they should ask other members in the class for help when they have a problem. They should know that all students are teachers, learners, and leaders and that all learners should ask for help when needed. If a student continues to interrupt the teacher during group work, set up an observation chair for the learner. He or she should sit in the chair until you are able to deal with the individual problem.

SNAPSHOT OF APPLICATION OF INSTRUCTIONAL COMPONENTS IN A CLASSROOM

Each day looks different in a multi-age active learning environment. It is sometimes difficult for an outsider to capture the whole picture of all of the unique components. This snapshot describes only segments of learning opportunities that can be seen in the classrooms.

Ms. Crumb is the head teacher for the "Detective" group, grades 2 and 3 multi-age classroom. The Voyagers have been studying about different types of communities for the past three weeks. Throughout the study, students have focused on distinguishing between urban, suburban, and rural communities. Living in a suburban environment, students are familiar with small towns, houses, and malls for shopping. In contrast to that, students took a trip to a rural town to pick apples and pumpkins and observe and collect data on what the term "rural community" means to them.

Students read and researched about cities on the Internet, gaining information on tall buildings, public transportation, commuters, museums, shopping venues, and sports areas. This data was used to establish a PBL project. Some students worked on generating murals of the data collected on different communities. Other students worked on a community skit or designed and constructed a digital community ecosystem. It is important to understand that students continue to make connections based on their own experiences and they build on their knowledge through an active learning environment between students to students and teacher to students.

A mini lesson is sometimes conducted as a literacy block early in the day, so that multi-age students have opportunities to apply the reading, writing, listening, and speaking skills in all the daily tasks whether based on the unit of study or not. A literacy workshop lesson targets all students in the class.

On this particular day, the workshop lesson objective is to teach main idea and details. Students use a passage from an informational text that describes what it is like to live in cities. The teacher models what the main idea is in the passage and one student points out a detail that supports the main idea. After this modeling session, students are asked to work with a partner to select a book on cities and find an example of a main idea with supporting details in one chapter of the book. They are asked to record their ideas on a graphic organizer.

Also, after the task is complete, each student records their ideas in journals and at the end of the session, partners share their findings with the whole class to determine if each partner group was able to successfully identify the appropriate data for the task. Ms. Crumb uses the graphic organizer, observation notes, and personal journals of students to determine which learners need more help.

Fluid groups are formed for students that need help and the teacher explains the main idea concept with the fluid group by practicing it by reading a book that is at the learners' independent reading levels. Then, students read independently and the small groups continue to be fluid.

Independent work is always encouraged by Ms. Crumb. Some students are writing books in the writing center. Others are constructing future cities using Legos and computer software. This learning environment is interactive for all learners to stay engaged in their learning.

EDUCATOR'S REFLECTION

This chapter has outlined lesson components that work in a multi-age program: the teacher directed workshop model, fluid grouping, PBL, independent learning, and learning centers. When implemented, these instructional components may look different for different classrooms. The teacher should consider these ideas and apply these elements to fit into each unique learning environment. What this chapter presents to the reader is a framework for applying the multi-age learning environment into school systems. This framework adapts well to all learners.

APPLICATION OF CONCEPTS FOR ALL SCHOOL SYSTEMS

All school programs should encourage the following:

- Instructional components of teacher directed workshop model, fluid grouping, PBL, independent learning, and learning centers should be implemented in all classrooms.

- Fluid groups should be used to target the needs of learners.
- Scaffolding and differentiated strategies should be applied and embedded ongoing in the learning environment and should not be isolated learning tasks.
- Independent learning experiences should be encouraged based on theme topics and student interest.
- Teachers should collaborate to plan and team teach as much as possible.

REFERENCES

Barell, J. (2010). *Problem-based learning: An inquiry approach* (2nd ed.). Thousand Oaks, CA: Corwin.

Bender, W. N. (2012). *Project-based learning: Differentiating instruction for the 21st century.* Thousand Oaks, CA: Corwin.

Burns, M. (2007). *About teaching mathematics: A K–8 resource.* Sausalito, CA: Math Solutions.

Calkins, L. (2001). *The art of teaching reading.* New York, NY: Longman.

Cleary, B. (2006). *Mouse and the motorcycle.* New York, NY: HarperCollins.

Cole, J. E., & Washburn-Moses, L. H. (2010). Going beyond "the math wars." A special educator's guide to understanding and assisting with inquiry-based teaching in mathematics. *Teaching Exceptional Children, 42*(4), 14–21.

Grant, M. M. (2010). Getting a grip on project-based learning: Theory, cases and recommendations. Retrieved from www.ncsu.edu/meridian/winn2002/514/3.html

Hall, T., Strangman, N., & Meyer, A. (2003). Differentiated instruction and implications for UDL implementation. Effective classroom practices report. Wakefield, MA: National Center on Accessing the General Curriculum.

Kaplan, S., Kaplan, J., Madsen, S., & Gould, B. (1980). *Change for children: Ideas and activities for individualizing learning.* Glenview, IL: Scott Foresman.

National Association for the Education of Young Children. (2009). *Developmentally appropriate early childhood programs serving children from birth through age 8.* Position paper. NAEYC. Retrieved from www.naeyc.org

Raphael, T. (1982). Question-answering strategies for children. *Reading Teacher, 36,* 186–190.

Richardson, J. (2009). *The next step in guided reading: Focused assessments and targeted lessons for helping every student become a better reader.* New York, NY: Scholastic.

Siena, M. (2009). *From reading to math: How best practices in literacy can make you a better math teacher.* Sausalito, CA: Math Solutions.

Tomlinson, C. A. (2005). *How to differentiate instruction in mixed-ability classrooms* (2nd ed.). Upper Saddle River, NJ: Pearson Education.

Tomlinson, C. A. (2014). *The differentiated classroom: Responding to the needs of all learners.* Alexandria, VA: ASCD.

Tomlinson, C. A., & Imbeau, M. B. (2010). *Learning and managing a differentiated classroom.* Alexandria, VA: ASCD.

6

Teaching Reading and Mathematics to Multi-Age Learners

Multi-age professional development is an ongoing process. Elenora, a teacher leader and Investigators (4–5) classroom teacher in the Discovery School, asked some questions during a professional development planning meeting: "How do I plan for a 4–5 group of students? Do I follow the grade textbook scope and sequence for each grade level? How do I support collaboration with a team of teachers during our planning sessions with curriculum maps?" Ms. George, the principal of the school, also had some questions: "How does an administrator support the teachers—what exactly are school leaders looking for that are effective ways to teach students? How do teachers accommodate students' needs in different subject areas??"

The questions are representative of just what educators think about when taking on a multi-age learning environment. Teachers and administrators are often confused as to how to plan and implement a quality curriculum for a multi-age group of learners. They find that it is overwhelming to consider Common Core State Standards and connect these standards to the diverse age groups. In this chapter, curriculum planning with Common Core State Standards is center to all planning and implementation of units and lessons.

Chapter 6 outlines how to curriculum plan for different ages in reading, writing, and mathematics and consider what the learning environment looks like. One question that is considered is the following: What do Reading Workshop, Math Workshop, and Writing Workshop look like in a multi-age setting?

CURRICULUM PLANNING WITH STANDARDS

To cover every subject's state standards, it would take a student moving through the K–12 education system at least 23 academic school years (Marzano, 2003). If teachers understand how to integrate standards with the planning process, they also know which standards are important to integrate in the learning process.

However, a learning organization has no real documentation (other than a teacher planning book) of what each teacher has included or excluded in the classroom planning process. What one teacher values, another teacher may not. The answer lies in the curriculum mapping process.

CURRICULUM MAPPING
PROCESS FOR MULTI-AGE LEARNING

Curriculum maps have two purposes in this program: the map is an ongoing collaborative process that targets curriculum and assessment; and, encourages measurable improvement in student performance (Jacobs, 2004). Multi-age school teams engage in explicit schoolwide planning because each school has increased accountability for multi-age student performance. For teachers, the exact process of planning is often quite fuzzy when dealing with multi-ages.

Curriculum mapping allows principals, teacher leaders, teachers, coaches, and professional developers to periodically review maps to gain an understanding of just what all teachers are doing with students. These maps can be adapted at any time during the school year.

A Collegial Process

Teachers are curriculum experts in the MAC program. For curriculum mapping to be an effective tool, teachers actively work together to advance one another's educational performance in multi-age classrooms and encourage a student's success. These teachers work together and collectively strive for better solutions and best practices to offer quality units and lessons so that all students are able to learn. Integrating this mapping process allows teachers, teacher leaders, and administrators to think, plan, act, and reflect ongoing to improve students' learning.

This team is responsible for designing and documenting curriculum goals and objectives such as making collegial curriculum decisions based on evidence; meet during PLC time based on multi-age teams, design interdisciplinary configurations; and, support upper and lower school committee agendas. The planning teams have one overarching goal: to target a better understanding of student learning needs. Fully disclosing one teacher's learning curriculum and practices is an important element to the curriculum mapping process. Everyone in the school community needs to share ideas to make this planning process effective (Hale, 2008).

Curriculum Maps

Curriculum maps are generated by all multi-age teachers before the school year begins. Teachers are asked to plan for at least three months when beginning the planning process. Teachers work in multi-age teams to look at each discipline and how to design interdisciplinary units that work across age groups and school levels. Teachers commonly begin by recording the following initial elements on a curriculum map (Jacobs, 2004):

- **Essential Topics to Cover:** Unit topic or subject area topic is targeted
- **Standards:** Proficiency targets that serve as a framework for what students need to know and do—teachers use three grade levels for planning
- **Content:** What students must know in subject areas
- **Concepts:** Ideas connected to what students should know
- **Assessment:** Use of formative assessment to find out what students know
- **Skills:** What do students do in relation to what they need to know?
- **Activities:** What do students need to do?
- **Active Learning:** Describe active learning strategies, child-centered, and project-based tasks
- **Academic Vocabulary:** Vocabulary that students should know
- **Higher-Level Thinking:** Bloom/Anderson Taxonomy and Webb's Depth of Knowledge integrated
- **Technology:** Technology use in lessons
- **Resources:** Materials and books needed for curriculum implementation

Elements on the map are not meant to be perceived as a sequential requirement. These ideas should only be used as a guide for teachers to follow. Teachers begin with designing units of study based on essential questions that support this planning process. Aligning standards to curriculum maps and developing essential questions is included in the initial mapping process. Essential questions are generated to connect to the content. The essential questions are open-ended, engaging, encourage higher-level thinking, sometimes point to other subject areas, raise other questions for inquiry, require evidence, and recur over time (McTighe & Wiggins, 2013). Some examples are: What do effective problem solvers do when they can't find a way to solve the problem? What are some connections between fiction and truth in stories?

Content describes the subject matter and can be a topic, theme, unit of study, or concept. Teachers in the MAC program use three grade levels of standards for the topic of study. For example, writing standards for the Explorers class (K–1) are as follows:

- **Kindergarten:** Use a combination of drawing, dictating, and writing to compose opinion pieces.

- **Grade 1:** Write informative/explanatory texts in which they name a topic and supply facts.
- **Grade 2:** Write informative/explanatory texts in which they introduce a topic, use facts and definitions to develop points (CCSS, 2010).

This alignment of three levels of the standards happens to be a very important component to consider in a multi-age class because it helps with planning for the diverse students' needs. Concepts break down the content area to a more specific category—for example, the content strand of algebraic relationships can be easily connected to the concept of pattern and relationships.

An assessment component requires teachers to document all the ways they assess their students for understanding of content, concepts, skills, and academic standards. Assessments in this program include performance assessments, products, and formative evaluation strategies such as journaling, exit slips, rubrics. Other assessment strategies will be discussed in chapter 7. Skills are looked at as the processes that students must use to understand the academic content and concepts.

For example, some mathematical process skills are: the application of problem solving or communicating ideas while finding mathematical solutions. Furthermore, activities are always tied to standards and they help students learn. Examples of activities are the following: form a poetry circle, create a bubble map showing photosynthesis, or make a table to solve a mathematics problem.

All activities should be interactive in nature that encourages student to student interaction and project-based tasks. Students should take the lead and the teacher is facilitator. Academic vocabulary is always introduced with each lesson and teachers are asked to keep a word wall of all important vocabulary words. Word walls help students to understand words related to units of study and help learners to use these words in tasks across the curriculum areas.

To combine levels of rigor, higher-level thinking processes are based on Bloom's Taxonomy (Andersen et al., 2001) and Webb's Depth of Knowledge (Blackburn, 2014). Bloom's Taxonomy allows the teacher to plan lessons that accommodate different thinking levels and Webb's Depth of Knowledge matrix assists teachers to plan the depth in which students need to engage with content to complete an assignment (see table 6.1). High-level thinking processes are integrated by all teachers in MAC when going through the curriculum mapping and planning sessions.

These thinking categories are used to encourage rigor and higher-level thinking when aligning curriculum, objectives, standards, and assessments. Multi-age curriculum maps (see table 6.2) and lesson plans (see table 6.3) come in many forms integrating the categories necessary for planning.

In these examples of curriculum planning maps and lessons, teachers use mapping components as needed.

Table 6.1. Bloom's Taxonomy and Webb's Depth of Knowledge

Revised Bloom's Taxonomy	Behaviors	Webb's Depth of Knowledge	Behaviors
Remembering	Recall information	Recall and reproduction	Recall a fact, information, or procedure
Understanding	Grasp the meaning of material	Skill/concept	Engage mental processes beyond habitual response using information or conceptual knowledge (sometimes requires two or more steps)
Applying	Use learned material in new and concrete ways	Strategic thinking	Requires reasoning, develop a plan or a sequence of steps
Analyzing	Break down material into parts so that the framework may be understood		
Evaluating	Make judgments based on criteria and standards	Extended thinking (correlates to Bloom's two highest levels)	Requires investigation, complex reasoning, planning, developing, and thinking—probably over an extended period of time
Creating	Put elements together to form a whole; reorganize elements into a new pattern or structure through generating, planning, producing		

Source: Adapted from Hess, Carlock, Jones, & Walkup (2009).

Table 6.2. Curriculum Map Upper School

Components for Mapping	October	November	December	Standards
Essential Questions or Topics to Cover	How does the global warming of the United States affect the environment of the country? Do ecological climate changes affect living conditions of people?	How has global warming affected people's exposure to the sun? How are families changed by their interaction with the new climate conditions?	Has global warming led to more cases for skin cancer? Has global warming led to more draughts?	1
Core Standards	6-8.1 Cite specific textual evidence to support analysis of science and technical texts. 6-8.2 Determine the central ideas or conclusions of a text; provide an accurate summary of the text distinct from prior knowledge or opinions. 6-8.3 Follow precisely a multistep procedure when carrying out experiments, taking measurements, or performing technical tasks.	6-8.1 Cite specific textual evidence to support analysis of science and technical texts. 6-8.2 Determine the central ideas or conclusions of a text; provide an accurate summary of the text distinct from prior knowledge or opinions. 6-8.3 Follow precisely a multistep procedure when carrying out experiments, taking measurements, or performing technical tasks.	6-8.1 Cite specific textual evidence to support analysis of science and technical texts. 6-8.2 Determine the central ideas or conclusions of a text; provide an accurate summary of the text distinct from prior knowledge or opinions. 6-8.3 Follow precisely a multistep procedure when carrying out experiments, taking measurements, or performing technical tasks.	3
Content	Earth Sciences (US) overview of content	Affects: Personal Health, Climate	Consequences	1
Concepts	Excess hydrocarbons create greenhouse effect. Greenhouse effect leads to global warming.	Culture and human activities are influenced by environmental conditions. Government policy influences environments impacts.	Climate changes affect culture and social relationships. Climate change affect economic conditions.	
Process Skills	Measure, collect data, record data	Research, collect, record, interpret data, classify, make a model, observe	Communicate, present findings	

Assessments	Maps, concept maps, science logs, major test	Competing theories on global warming, climate charts, Essay: Global warming—Fact or Fiction	Greenhouse effect demonstration, Student presentations	1, 2
Activities	Classify objects, video on debates over global warming	Lab experiments to model global warming and greenhouse effect	Lab experiments to model health effects of depleted ozone	1, 2
Describe Active Learning Strategies, Child-centered, Project-based Tasks	"The Climate and Me" Sheets, Ball-Toss Name Game, Textbook Scavenger hunts, US Physical and climate maps, Pictures from satellites, Intro to Laptops—Journey through climate change—the past 10,000 years	Internet research site, major test—Earth Science, Pictures from definitions; Video—the climate in the year 2100; Begin research on Discovery Channel PowerPoint	Brochure—Region Project Turn in on Discovery Channel PowerPoint; Field trip to Earth Science Museum	1, 2
Vocabulary	Climate, hydrocarbons, carbon emissions, weather	Artic, atmosphere, climate, solar radiation	Solar energy, greenhouse, effect, fossil fuels	1, 2
Resources Used	Videos, websites, pictorials	Videos, websites, pictorials	Videos, websites, pictorials	1, 2
Higher-Level Thinking (Bloom/Andersen / Webb Framework)	Knowledge (remembering), comprehension (understanding); Evaluating and Creating	Application (implementing), analysis (organizing); Evaluating and Creating	Synthesis (creating), evaluation (critiquing)	1, 2
Technology	Earth Science Video, Laptops—Discovery Channel, Brochure—Climate, Word Documents	Videos, Lab demonstrations, Word Documents	Videos, Discovery PowerPoint Project	3
Miscellaneous Notations	N/A	N/A	N/A	

Table 6.3. Multi-Age Lesson Plan Lower School

LESSON TOPICS
English Language Arts & Reading

Unit Essential Questions
1. What is going to happen next in the story?
2. Do you think mice really have beds and, if so, what are they made of?
3. If you were the boy, how would you feel?
4. If you were the mouse, explain why you would want a certain thing and what you would do with it?

Common Core State Standards
RL 1.1 Ask and answer questions about key details in a text.
RL 1.2 Retell stories, including key details, and demonstrate understanding of their central message or lesson.
RL 2.1 Ask and answer such questions as who, what, where, when, why, and how to demonstrate understanding of key details in a text.
RL 2.3 Describe how characters in a story respond to major events and challenges.
RL.K.7 With prompting and support, describe the relationship between illustrations and the story in which they appear (e.g., what moment in a story an illustration depicts).
RL.K.9 With prompting and support, compare and contrast the adventures and experiences of characters in familiar stories.
RL.K.10 Actively engage in group reading activities with purpose and understanding.

Lesson Objectives
Students will:
• Practice critical thinking by predicting what will happen next in the story
• Identify the cause-effect relationship of story events
• Practice speaking skills by presenting their own version of the story to the class
• Demonstrate comprehension of cause-effect relationships by creating a story which has a sequence of cause-effect events

Assessments
1. Satisfactory: "If . . . , then . . . " statement represents a direct cause-effect relationship.
2. Not Satisfactory: "If . . . , then . . . " statement does not represent a direct cause-effect relationship.
3. Assess each student's knowledge and interpretation of the cause-effect relationship through the student's own story. These stories should present clear examples of cause-effect relationships using "if . . . , then . . . " statements that make sense to the reader.

Step-by-Step Lesson Procedures and Tasks

SESSION 1

1. Seat students together at the shared reading carpet, asking the students if they like cookies. Then ask the students what is their favorite kind of cookie.
2. Show students the cover of *If You Give a Mouse a Cookie* and ask students to read the title of the book and look at the picture on the cover, asking, "What do you think this story is saying about a mouse and a cookie?"
3. Take students on a picture walk, pausing to allow time for them to discuss, and share unfamiliar vocabularies.
4. Have the students relate their own experiences to the title, asking, "What do you have with your cookie?"
5. Ask the students to predict what is going to happen next in the story. Write down the predictions.
6. Read the book aloud to the students. Stop to check predictions and make new ones.
7. At the end, to reinforce the story's circular structure, asking "What do you think will happen if the mouse is given another cookie?"

SESSION 2

1. Play the video story of *If You Give a Mouse a Cookie* to the students.
2. After watching the video, teach vocabularies.

SESSION 3

1. Distribute the Story Circle handout, scissors, and sentence strips to students. Instruct students to cut out each story card and place it in order of the story sequence.
2. Encourage students to discuss with each other about the order of the story.
3. When the sentence strip pictures are in the correct sequential order, asking students to glue them to the sentence strips.

SESSION 4

1. Ask learners with advanced comprehension skills and writing skills to create their own story instead of doing the Story Circle handout. Their story must have the cause-effect relationship and sentences like "if . . . , then . . . ."

SESSION 5

1. Have students share their stories with the class at the read-aloud area. Ask the author to refine their stories after listening to others' opinions.
2. Print out students' stories and put them in the mini-library for students to borrow after the class.
3. Publish good stories created by students online to share with parents.

(continued)

Table 6.3. *(Continued)*

Differentiated Instructional Practices
1. Students' assignments are organized and assigned based on ability and skill level.
2. Invite students to read their own story and record it by using a voice recorder or an iPad using interesting apps such as Talking Tom Cat.
3. Small copies of the story are placed on the iPad or the computer at the listening center and invite the children to read along with it at their leisure.
4. Place mouse and child hand puppets at the dramatic play center so that students can stage puppet shows based on the story or their own stories.
Higher-Level Thinking Critical-Thinking Skills Analytical Skills Synthesizing
Resources Needed • Story Circle handout: Students will use this handout to recall the events of the story and organize the matching picture cards into the story sequence. • *If You Give a Mouse a Cookie* by Laura Joffe Numeroff (Laura Geringer Publishers, 1985) • Large pieces of chart paper or whiteboard • Word and phrase cards • Chart paper • Scissors • Glue • Video Story *If You Give a Mouse a Cookie* • Computer • Projector

Source: Adapted from Bass (2013).

SNAPSHOT OF CURRICULUM MAPPING MEETING

It is summer and the teachers and administrators are meeting to discuss what they should plan for the coming school year. Teachers for all multi-age classes come together today to discuss how to plan mathematics content strands. Ellen, the teacher leader for the lower school, suggests that they plan for one month to begin the school year. All colleagues agree the first task for mapping will be to plan for the first month of the school year. They decide to begin with the strand Number and Operations.

Across grade levels the teachers decide on which concepts should be taught based on the core standards. Jarrett, the Quadrilaterals (grades 4–5) teacher states, "Children's math learning, no matter what age, should emphasize the development of number sense." Carry, the new teacher in the Hexagon (K–1) class, asks Jarrett to elaborate on what he means. Jarrett says, "We need to get our students in our multi-age learning community to see patterns and relationships among numbers, and we should encourage them to examine the properties of numbers."

Carry responds by saying, "I only teach 5- and 6-year-olds. They can't do those things with numbers." Kevin, the teacher leader for the upper school mathematics program, jumps into the conversation by saying, "We have to get our children to investigate the use of numbers in many situations so that they develop the confidence and flexibility to apply their understandings. On your Hexagon (K–1) level you should get your young students to study patterns." Jarrett jumps in and says, "The exploration of patterns in numerical relationships needs to be an ongoing part of the elementary mathematics program for all of our multi-age students."

Kevin states, "In the upper school, students investigate whether numbers are prime or composite, whether they are even or odd. In the lower school, young students create color number bracelets by choosing three color beads of blue, pink, and yellow. Teachers ask students to create a pattern of colors using a 1-2-3 pattern with the beads. For example, a pattern with beads might be: 1 pink, 2 blue, 3 yellow. Then, the young child must figure out how many beads are on the bracelet. For the Rectangles (2–3) learners, young children choose any two numbers for 0 to 9 and follow this rule: add the two numbers and record just the digit that appears in the ones place in the sum. If a learner starts with 8 and 9, then the next number would be 7."

"Whatever we plan, I think our team agrees that we need to embed problem solving situations into mathematics teaching and learning," said Jarrett. "Yes, yes, yes, . . . I get it!" exclaimed Carry. "Can we only map out mathematics ideas for the month of September and then meet again to share what we planned?" Jarrett smiled and said, "Yes, I agree, let us meet next Tuesday."

The curriculum map meeting helps teacher to share ideas about how mathematics concepts connect to different levels of student learning. It also allows educators in a school to share their expertise and help other colleagues.

READING, WRITING, AND MATH WORKSHOPS IN A MULTI-AGE SETTING

A term we use in the MAC program often is the *workshop model* that was defined extensively in chapter 5. In this chapter, a discussion connects the workshop model within the multi-age teaching and learning framework with reading, writing, and mathematics. In the multi-age classroom, the workshop is a place where students are always engaged in intensive tasks to assist them in understanding the content, concepts, and skills in all disciplines.

There is an understanding (in all classrooms of the program) that learners will be involved in active learning by doing hands on tasks, collaborating on projects, and sharing their ideas with others. Teachers encourage students to think that they are acting as "apprentices" to expert readers, writers, mathematicians, historians, scientists, and so on.

Multi-age classroom workshops may look a little different depending on the teacher, but they follow the same framework and include the components that were presented in chapter 5. All mini lessons begin with a short direct instruction presentation by the teacher. The presentation is followed with either collaborative work or independent tasks. The relative school day has a breakdown of time on task in specific ways (see figure 6.1).

The MAC program encourages teachers to use less time leading whole group lessons (30%) and more time on small group work when the teacher works with several students (20%). All lessons integrate group work (20%) to encourage learners to collaborate with other peers and share ideas. Students are often encouraged to work independently on assignments and projects (15%) during the school day.

Orbital study projects give choices to the student in selecting his or her own topics of study for independent work (10%). Moving between tasks and events during the day with transition time usually takes a small amount of time (5%) because the caring and trusting learning community is cohesive in nature with subject areas and class routines integrating in some way.

LITERACY WORKSHOP

Learners in the MAC program must have numerous opportunities to read and write during each day. The reading and writing materials are engaging and personally relevant for each multi-age learner. Each learner reads and writes independently on

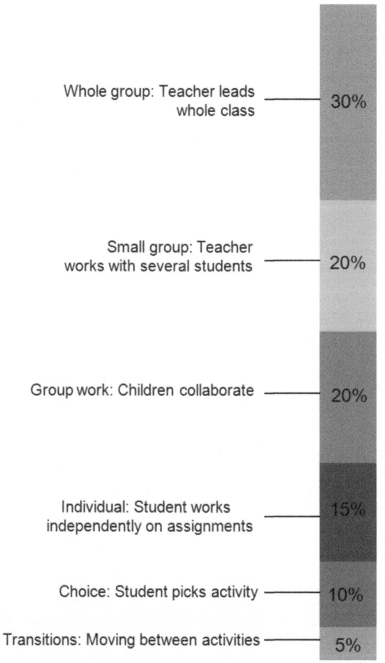

Figure 6.1. Relative School Day Breakdown in a Multi-Age Classroom

an ongoing basis. The literacy goals for learning are based on Common Core State Standards (2010) for all multi-age learning communities as per the following:

- To become competent learners in decoding and encoding information.
- To gain necessary strategies for comprehending a wider range of literary genres.
- To develop the ability to communicate and write about reading and writing.
- To make reading and writing lifelong tasks.

Multi-age community reading has two purposes: to provide every learner with access to age appropriate vocabulary, concepts, and language structures; and, to create context that support the development of the multi-age classroom as a learning community where learners of mixed ability levels interact and learn from one another.

Reading Lesson Components

Students read the same text, or a collection of texts, about the same theme during a teacher directed lesson in a multi-age reading workshop. This lesson begins with a teacher directed lesson during which a concept is taught. Learners prepare for reading by making predictions, reviewing new vocabulary, gaining an understanding of a new reading process concept, and asking questions. The teacher allocates about 15–20 minutes to the teacher directed component. Then, learners break into small groups or partnerships to read the text and complete teacher-assigned cooperative learning tasks based on the concepts and vocabulary taught in the teacher directed lesson.

The task is selected to motivate learners to reflect on and respond to the text in ways that clarify meaning through application of ideas. For example, after a teacher directed workshop lesson on main idea and details, the learners work on story maps by constructing a folded book that depicts the main idea on the first page and details on the following pages. The learners are also engaged in rigorous tasks by asking students to make connections to character's actions and story outcomes. Some questions that learners think about are: What if the character had acted differently? How would these actions have changed the ending of the story?

For some students, the teacher may assist struggling readers that find the text at a *frustration level* for reading. The teacher intervenes and creates a small group of learners and uses strategies that make the text readable for these students such as: read all or part of the text aloud before children are expected to read on their own; assign buddy reading; or, present vocabulary ongoing that is essential to comprehend the text.

After all learners have read and responded to the text, the groups all respond in individual journals about the lesson by answering the following prompts: What did you learn? What were some challenges? Then, the learners reconvene as a multi-age class to share and discuss the small heterogeneous groups' solutions.

Strategies for Teaching Reading

The close reading method, guided reading framework, and literacy circles connect to workshop sessions so that all multi-age learners receive the most effective strategies to assist learners to become successful readers. *Spot On* and *Solo Reading* that are adapted from Paratore and McCormack (2005) include *just-right* reading and *on-your-own reading*. These strategies fit into the workshop model very easily.

Close Reading

Must everyone read the same book in a multi-age classroom? The answer is yes, at least at certain times. In the MAC program, we think that there are many benefits when learners share a common reading experience when reading the same book. First, it is hard to encourage the learning community atmosphere without such reading time. It is also important to make sure that when learners are asked to read challenging books that are not on an instructional or independent level, we need to have conversation, guidance, and interaction with all learners (Pasquarelli, 2006).

However, teachers should choose the book wisely for the group. Think of the learners and try to find a book that meets the needs for all multi-age students. The book should not have difficult vocabulary and multiple shifts in points of view. A teacher should be prepared to help learners in multiple ways. Some learners will need for the teacher to support their reading through read aloud moments, listen to the audio version of the book, or have learners buddy-read with a student. It is important that the teacher gives ongoing support to all readers.

Fluid Grouping, Guided Reading, and Literature Circles

Fluid groups in multi-age literacy classrooms are often structured around a variety of strategies such as Guided Reading and Literature Circles. These strategies are discussed next. Guided reading is a strategy that enables the teacher to view each learner's reading ability and give support to effectively support each learner's reading development.

Guided reading in multi-age classrooms should not be used to group learners by grade level to move them through a prescribed basal series. In the multi-age classroom, learners progress in reading at their own rates and do not compete with each other, but rather encourage each other during the learning process.

The selected text must be at the group's instructional level. Instructional-level texts are those that provide students with supports and only a few challenges. It should be that the selected text for the group offers a minimum number of new concepts, strategies, and skills necessary for the learners to grapple with (Schulman, 2006). The following is how this reading process is implemented in the multi-age classroom (Fisher & Frey, 2010; Richardson, 2009; Schulman, 2006):

- Select the text, focus, and purpose of the guided reading lesson: text should be on the instructional level of the guided reading group, and the focus for the lesson is the strategic plan—questioning, inferring, summarizing.
- The purpose for reading is when the teacher encourages learners to read to find out something about the focus in the text. For example, the focus of a lesson in a 2–3 group is to apply the inference skill. The teacher begins the silent reading

session by asking learners to look for clues that show evidence of what kind of person the main character might be. Learners are instructed to think about what the character says, does, and how he or she looks. The learners use inference clues to discuss the character after reading.

- Prior to reading, frontload the multi-age learners' knowledge of a text to assist with becoming actively involved in constructing meaning. This can be done by connecting to the learner's personal experiences, showing artifacts, reading aloud a picture book, or viewing a video. What learners know about the topic before reading the text will influence the reading process in a successful way. Also, the learners should skim the text and look for difficult vocabulary prior to reading.

Give directions of what students will do during the reading process. For example, the teacher will write on chart paper and read aloud the focus of the reading, in question form: "What inferences (clues) do you find that allow you to understand the kind of person the main character is in the story?" After the introduction of the text is complete, each learner reads the text. The teacher hands out sticky notes and asks learners to mark, code, and record important clues in the text that describe the character. Also, students record any vocabulary words which they struggle with.

Guided reading is not round robin reading. The learners in the group read silently and the teacher moves to each student to ask a learner to quietly read aloud a short passage. The teacher jots down observations of errors and corrections of each learner. The teacher focuses on some questions such as: How did you figure out what is going on with the character? How do you know this character feels the way it does? Can you read this short passage of what the character says and make it sound like the character? What words give you the most problem?

Teachers support competent readers and this process helps to do that. After reading, the teacher returns to the focus and asks students to have conversations about how they can answer the focus question. Learners place sticky notes on the chart paper to answer the original focus question. They discuss deeper ideas about the inferences or clues they found in the text.

Literature circles, another effective strategy for multi-age classrooms, can be interchanged with guided reading. Literature circle, a small group of learners that come together to discuss the same book, is as a way of deepening their literacy skills and understandings. The group ranges from four to six learners and usually forms around the students' choice of book that may be based on a topic of study or theme. *Spot On* reading is encouraged in the multi-age class in a literature circle format. *Spot On* reading is just right for the reader—the text can be read by the reader with 90–95% accuracy.

This literature group can be used during any part of the day. The teacher facilitates the literature groups by visiting each group, reading with them and asking probing questions that include rigorous thinking processes such as the following: Was there a lesson to be learned in the book? How did this story make you feel? Did the story make you think about something you have not thought about before? Are there words or phrases that help you understand the story? Also, the time allows the teacher to work one-on-one with a learner.

Older students read aloud to each other and discuss the book during literature time. Prior to the literature circle meeting, the teacher gives direction on what skill the group should be working on for the day such as finding inferences in the story that describe the main character. As the multi-age learners become more independent in the discussion process, the teacher allows them to direct the group. The group selects a leader and the group decides on the number of pages to read and discuss during the session.

Discussion of the book may also include the use of organizing the text information on a graphic organizer such as a character analysis chart. Younger children may meet in a literature circle with an older child or adult leading the group by reading the book aloud to them as they follow along. Then, the young children share and discuss the book together with guidance.

Solo read is independent reading that may take place at any time. The reading materials are on an independent reading level for the learner and each learner meets with the teacher to conference about the progress that has been made on a weekly basis.

Reading aloud to children should be done daily. During read aloud time, multi-age learners of mixed abilities enjoy listening to stories and informational text that capture their interests. Teachers model what reading should sound like through reading chapter books and picture books. Teachers are the primary readers, but "guest reader" is encouraged by allowing each student to read aloud for a session. In a multi-age class, guest readers can range from emergent to fluent readers. All levels of reading are supported by everyone. It is good to recommend that a guest reader (who is often a parent) uses a solo reading book to use during read aloud. This way the guest reader is familiar with the text that is shared.

Reading across the curriculum is an ongoing process in a multi-age classroom. If learners are studying ocean life, they read informational text and stories about ocean ecosystems. If they are studying poetry, they are reading poems. Project-based learning also offers opportunities for reading across the content areas. If learners are exploring a project on environmental issues than they will read for information, read what other learners write, and read for enjoyment. The focus for reading in a multi-age classroom is to develop reading skills by reading in meaningful ways.

Writing Workshop

The writing process is taught in a Writing Workshop. Our MAC program supports the notion that writing instruction should be structured around the standards the students need to meet and the genres that need to be taught (Pasquarelli, 2006). A typical writing workshop has five basic components: mini lesson, writing drafts, conferring, editing and publishing, and sharing as an author (Calkins, 2006).

The mini lesson is taught by the teacher for no more than 10 minutes. It is a teacher-directed lesson focusing on a strategy such as presenting informational text on birds to see how the author organizes factual information on the topic. The teacher might point to the table of contents, the chapters, and read a short passage of the text. The teacher points to how a student author may use the same components to make an informational text on his or her own topic of study. After the mini lesson, the writing time begins for the multi-age learners.

Learners can apply what they learned in the mini lesson to their own writing pieces, if they choose, or use the strategy in their writing at a later date. During writing time learners may conference with other students, teachers, or parents and also work collaboratively with others. Students also ask a buddy to help with the editing of the draft by sharing ideas and giving feedback. Learners may publish their work if the draft is complete.

At the end of writing workshop, the teacher chooses two or three students to share their work. The author sits in an author's chair to share with the group. Multi-age learners listen to the author sharing and then learners give feedback and ask questions to help with the writing piece. Final draft pieces or pieces in varying stages of development can be displayed in the classroom and in the halls. An author's tea session is scheduled once per month so that authors may share published work with other students, teachers, and parents. This is an excellent strategy to integrate parents into the learning process and encourage the caring and trusting ways of the program.

While thinking the yearlong curriculum on writing, we generally target the following main categories in the MAC program (Calkins, 2006): narratives, persuasive or expository essays, how-to text, informational writing, and poetry. In the primary school, persuasive essays are not usually emphasized. In the upper school, functional or how-to and procedural texts are used in math and science and other content areas (Calkins, 2006). It is important that teachers schedule writing workshop at least three times per week. It is hoped that writing workshop can happen daily. When multi-age children write as authors frequently, they become excellent writers in a short amount of time.

Writing workshop is an excellent strategy that supports multi-age writers. Younger learners may write three or four lines in a story, while older children may compose five or six paragraphs. No matter the stage of writing development of a learner, all learners can share together in writing workshop because everyone understands that they are authors and they are able to share ideas through writing. As a teacher edits with a learner during writing workshop, the child is nurtured to the next stage of writing based on individual needs. Learners also learn from other learners through listening and discussing writing samples of multi-age students, and reviewing sample writings that surface from writing workshop sessions.

Writing Across the Curriculum

Multi-age learners are encouraged not only to read, but also to write across the content areas. For example, students are always writing in personal journals after each lesson session. They reflect on what they learned and what challenges they had. For example, independent writing occurs at centers and in projects. When multi-age learners are studying about folk tales, they read folk talks and then write their own folk tales.

When they study about communities around the world, they research on the Internet and write about a community. If they investigate how to get a clay boat to float, they write about the results in a science log. If children explore multiplication sets using manipulatives at the mathematics center, they draw and write about how they solved the problems. The multi-age learners *write to learn* by writing for many purposes through open-ended experiences that give meaning to learning.

MATHEMATICS WORKSHOP

The goals in mathematic are similar to literacy. Learners need to do the following:

- Become literate in mathematical understandings in all content strands
- Be able to read mathematical situations and understand them
- Become skilled in using mathematics computations
- Use mathematical thinking to problem solve

We know that most mathematical topics are much too big to learn in one or two lessons. Learners need to explore the mathematics concepts over many days in numerous situations such as using collaborative groups to solve problems, integrate hands-on tasks with materials, and work independently on projects or in learning center activities.

A teacher-directed lesson in math class begins with the teacher introducing a concept. Teachers tend to have longer whole group lessons because extensive classroom discussions often surface based on topics. However, mini lessons are structured so that there is time after a teacher directed session to give opportunity for students to work in small groups, partnerships, or on their own (independent of their teacher). After these mini-lesson components are completed, each student reflects about the mathematics learning process by recording his or her ideas in a journal. Then each student shares solutions to the mathematics task with the whole class.

On day two, the teacher creates fluid groups based on each student's needs. The snapshot that follows describes what an observer might find in Day 1 and Day 2 of a mathematics workshop for multi-age learners.

SNAPSHOT OF A MATHEMATICS WORKSHOP

Maximus is a teacher for the Coaches (grades 4–5) mathematics class. He has been teaching for 4 years. He started teaching in a traditional classroom, but when he got the opportunity to join a multi-age school program, he jumped at the teaching job. He said he was excited to have a classroom that encouraged hands-on tasks with manipulatives and materials. He also thought that it was important for students to work in active classrooms by collaborating in groups and partnerships with other students. Most importantly, he thought that children at different ages pace themselves according to what they know already. He found in his past teaching that grade-level math concepts often do not fit the needs of all learners.

He was feeling very confident in using the workshop model to teacher math to his 4–5 multi-age students. He liked the lesson model that encourages teacher directed lessons followed by small group independent work. He also thought that the reflective journal writing piece in the lesson helped him to assess which students were having difficulty with understanding the lesson concepts and which students needed more challenging work with decimals.

Day 1: Maximus Reflects on His Teaching

"Before the lesson on the topic of 'decimals on grids,' I record on chart paper the Common Core State Standards which were the following: third grade standards: develop an understanding of fractions as numbers; fourth grade standards: use decimal notation for fractions with denominators 10 or 100. Fifth grade standards: read and write decimals to thousandths. These standards are listed from three different grade levels so that I am able to accommodate learners at all levels. Some students struggle with understanding just what a fraction stands for and other students are able to move to use decimal notation to represent a fraction or even read and write decimals in a variety of ways. Tomorrow we will split into small fluid groups based on what work we need to accomplish and I have also set up learning center independent menu activities. The centers will be used if learners are not with me working in a small group. I will explain more about the menu tasks tomorrow during Day 2 of our mathematics workshop."

He began to explain his lesson expectations to the students. The teacher stated, "Today we are going to learn about decimals." He reads from the chart paper the standards that the class will consider for the next few days of mathematics workshop. "If some of you find fractions difficult to understand, we will do more work with fractional parts. If others are ready we will move into lesson tasks that help you to see the relationship between decimals and common fractions. And, if others need to be challenged, we will look at tenths and hundredths in different ways."

Maximus mentions to students, "I have placed on your worktables the mathematics materials that are 10-by-10 grids with crayons and other materials that will help us visualize how we turn fractions into decimals."

Introduction of Teacher Directed Math Workshop Lesson

The teacher introduces decimal notation by beginning with tenths using the resource Marilyn Burns, *About Teaching Mathematics: A K–8 Resource* (Burns, 2007). On the Smart Board, there are several 10 x 10 grids. The teacher talks to the students about the grids by pointing out the number of small squares, columns, and rows. On one grid the teacher asks students to shade four columns of squares and asks, "What fractional part of the grid is shaded?" Learners begin to respond with four-tenths or forty-hundredths. The teacher models this and then asks why this makes sense. Then, the teacher shows learners how to record fractions as decimals: 0.4 and 0.40. The discussion begins as to why there are differences between the two numerals. The teacher continues with other examples until learners begin to show understanding.

Working in Collaborative Groups: Students are placed in heterogeneous groups of four that integrate learners of mixed abilities and mixed ages. Each group is given a blank 10-by-10 grid, and asked to make up their own problems by shading any amount they like on the grid and record different ways to record symbolically the portion of the grid they shade. Once groups are ready, they share their solutions and discuss ideas with the whole class. Jamie, a 9-year-old, shares his group's solution: "We colored eight small squares and we wrote it as 8/10 or 0.8." The teacher asks the class if this solution makes sense. If they agree, they hold up thumbs; if they disagree they hold their thumbs down. This simple process allows the teacher to see which individual student is unable to understand the concepts at this point in the lessons.

Reflective Journal Writing in a Personal Journal: At the end of the lesson session each learner writes what he or she learned in the lesson and what were some of the challenges. Allen writes, "I don't know what I am doing!!! I just don't get it. When I color three columns of squares, why is this thirty-hundredths?" He shares this with the class during a voluntary journal read aloud. Alex, a 10-year-old, responds by saying, "Cause three columns are shaded on a big square of a hundred squares." Allen yells, "Oh . . . now I get . . . a big square!" This reflective journal is just another excellent strategy for assessing individual understanding.

Debrief/Share: Each group shares their solutions and the whole class discusses if the solutions are the best answers.

Day 2: Mathematics Workshop Fluid Grouping

The next day, following the teacher directed workshop lesson, the teacher reviews the assessment strategies and decides which students need extra work in the following areas: more work needed on understanding fractions; more work on understanding decimals with tenths and hundredths; or, need to move on to more challenging concepts. The teacher meets in small groups with each group. One group builds rectangles with color tiles and grid paper to build a rectangle that is 1/2 red, 1/4 yellow, and 1/4 green. Another group continues with other examples of tenths and hundredths on grids. Another group explores some ways to extend the previous day's lesson by writing mixed numerals such as using three grids to show 3 3/10, 3.3.

Learning Centers

As each small multi-age group meets with the teacher, other multi-age groups are working on independent work in learning centers. The Menu for the learning center tasks varies. Activities target the concepts that are covered in the workshops. This particular Learning Center Menu targets fractions and decimals. These menu tasks allow learners to continue to explore fractions and decimals on a variety of levels.

Prior to the independent session, the teacher creates a menu for each learner to differentiate the learning process for each student. Students select specific menu tasks based on what they can do independently without support from the teacher. However, if learners have questions during independent work, the students are allowed to ask other students for help. Some menu tasks that were implemented by Maximus, the teacher, were based on using the resource Marilyn Burns, *About Teaching Mathematics: A K–8 Resource* (Burns, 2007). Teachers do not always reinvent the wheel to create multi-age tasks. Teachers are always encouraged to use a variety of resources to help with planning stages. Maximus sets up the following centers:

- **Decimals in the Newspaper:** Look for articles in which decimals are used. Choose one to post on the center board and explain the meaning of the decimal.
- **Write Mixed Numerals Using Grids:** Use grids to write mixed numerals using three grids: For example, use three grids to show 2 3/10 or 2.3. Create four examples of mixed numerals.
- **Comparing Decimals:** Use grids to compare decimal numerals. Students use pairs of decimal numerals to compare, or have several numerals to put in order, such as 0.14, 0.2, 0.47, and 0.3.

- **Build the Yellow Hexagon:** Using pattern blocks, find all the different ways you can build the yellow hexagon from different assortments of blocks. Count only different combinations of blocks.

Debrief/Share

At the end of the mathematics fluid group sessions, students come together on the rug to share what they completed for the day. The independent learning center tasks are kept in a folder for the teacher to review later.

This mathematics workshop framework described in this snapshot is an excellent example of how mathematics is taught in a multi-age learning environment. The description defines that the math workshop components allow teachers to target the needs of all learners based on the individual needs of each student.

EDUCATOR'S REFLECTION

Curriculum mapping prior to the school year is an essential process for multi-age classrooms. This process allows teachers, teacher leaders, and administrators to collectively make decisions on what should be taught during the school year. It is a planning time that places curriculum ideas on paper. These maps can be changed at any time. Maps should be periodically reviewed to gain an understanding of what all teachers are doing in multi-age classrooms.

Reading/writing and mathematics workshops integrate many components that assist teachers to target the needs of each learner. Students are encouraged to be active learners. The program encourages students to think as if they are "apprentices" to expert readers, writers, and mathematicians. Workshop formats may look different depending on the teacher, but most strategies are integrated into classroom lessons. In reading, there are many effective strategies used: close reading, guided reading, fluid grouping, solo reading, reading across the curriculum, and independent reading.

In writing workshop, learners become authors using the writing process to guide their personal narratives, persuasive essays, how-to-text, informational writing, and poetry. A tea party celebration with parents and the school community conclude monthly student author publications. This type of event integrates the caring and trusting elements that are found throughout the multi-age learning community.

Mathematics workshop encourages mathematics problem solving, skill understandings, and computational procedural knowledge. This is done with group work, fluid groups, whole class instruction, and learning centers. All students learn in this multi-age teaching and learning community because teachers target each student's learning needs in meaningful ways.

APPLICATION OF CONCEPTS FOR ALL SCHOOL SYSTEMS

All school programs should encourage the following:

- Curriculum mapping is an essential process that should be done in a collective manner before the school year begins.
- Reading, writing, and mathematics should use a variety of strategies to target learners—whole group, fluid groups, independent work, and learning centers.
- Learners should be involved in active learning environments that encourage inquiry, problem solving, hands-on tasks, and independent learning.

REFERENCES

Anderson, L. W., & Krathwohl, D. R. (2000). *A taxonomy for learning, teaching, and assessing: A revision of Bloom's Taxonomy of educational objectives.* New York, NY: Addison Wesley Longman.

Anderson, L. W., Krathwohl, D. R., Airasian, P. W., Cruikshank, K. A., Mayer, R. E., Pintrich, P. R., et al. (Eds.). (2001). *A taxonomy for learning, teaching, and assessing: A revision of Bloom's Taxonomy of educational objectives.* Boston, MA: Allyn and Bacon.

Bass, L. (2013). Integrating language arts: *If You Give a Mouse a Cookie.* International Literacy Association. Retrieved from http://www.readwritethink.org/classroom-resources/lesson-plans/integrating-language-arts-give-809.html

Blackburn, B. R. (2014). *Rigor in the classroom: A toolkit for teachers.* New York, NY: Routledge.

Burns, M. (2007). *About teaching mathematics: A K–8 resource.* Sausalito, CA: Math Solutions.

Calkins, L. (2006). *A guide to the writing workshop, grades 3–5.* Portsmouth, NH: Heinemann.

Common Core State Standards Initiative. (2010). Retrieved from http://www.corestandards.org

Fisher, D., & Frey, N. (2010). *Guided instruction: How to develop confident and successful learners.* Alexandria, VA: Association of Supervision and Curriculum Development.

Hale, J. A. (2008). *A guide to curriculum mapping; Planning, implementing, and sustaining the process.* Thousand Oaks, CA: Corwin Press.

Hess, K., Carlock, D., Jones, B., & Walkup, J. (2009). What exactly do "fewer, clearer, and higher standards" really look like in the classroom? Using a cognitive rigor matrix to analyze curriculum, plan lessons, and implement assessments. Presentation at CCSSO, Detroit, MI, June 2009. Retrieved from http://www.nciea.org/cgi-bin/pubspage.cgi?sortby=pub_date

Jacobs, H. H. (2004). *Getting results with curriculum mapping.* Alexandria, VA: Association for Supervision and Curriculum Development.

Marzano, R. J. (2003). *What works in schools: Translating research into action.* Alexandria, VA: Association for Supervision and Curriculum Development.

McTighe, J., & Wiggins, G. (2013). *Essential questions: Opening doors to student understanding.* Alexandria, VA: Association for Supervision and Curriculum Development.

Paratore, J. R., & McCormack, R. L. (2005). *Teaching literacy in second grade.* New York, NY: Guilford Press.

Pasquarelli, S. L. (2006). The practice of teaching genre by genre. In S. L. Pasquarelli (Ed.), *Teaching writing genres across the curriculum: Strategies for middle school teachers* (pp. 1–14). Greenwich, CT: Information Age.

Richardson, J. (2009). *The next step in guided reading: Focused assessments and targeted lessons for helping every student become a better reader.* New York, NY: Scholastic.

Schulman, M. B. (2006). *Guided reading in grades 3–6: Everything you need to make small-group reading instruction work in your classroom.* New York, NY: Scholastic.

7

Curriculum Cycles, Interdisciplinary Studies, and Other Effective Strategies in the Multi-Age Classroom

Mary Kay, the Poets (grades 2–3) teacher, asked her PLC to focus their meeting agenda on a very important question that she continues to grapple with: How do we use mandated social studies and science curricula that are tied to grade level topics in a multi-age classroom? Jake, the Authors (K–1) teacher, mentioned that he also struggled with this issue. He asked the team, "What do we do with a curriculum designating that first graders study animals, magnets, and the family; second graders, plants, weather, and local communities; and third graders, rocks, electricity, and global communities? These topics can take much time during the school year and we can't teach it all."

DEVELOPING CURRICULUM CYCLES

Working with separate topics or themes based on each grade level in social studies and science defeats the purpose for implementing a multi-age learning community. For social studies and science, the multi-age teacher's approach is to select specific themes that connect to the grade-level topics.

One solution is to focus on developing *curriculum cycles* that repeat themes every fourth year. This design plan of curricula will eliminate having multi-age students repeat the same topics of study each year. The following social studies and science list is one way a MAC PLC developed themes for 6- to 8-year-olds. The teachers considered the grade-level topics and generated the curriculum cycles plan for a 3-year period (see table 7.1).

This curriculum cycle is always considered when planning for social studies and science. These topics are selected based on social studies and science curriculum. There is no set rule on how many themes should be planned for the year and how

Table 7.1.   Topics (Themes) of Study for a Three-Year Cycle

Year of Study	Topic (Theme) of Study
Year 1	Animals native to the local area
	Ocean life
	Magnets
	Human body
	Ecosystems
	Ancient Egypt
Year 2	Insects and the lifecycle
	Plants
	Food and nutrition
	Electricity
	Colonial life in America
Year 3	Prehistoric life
	Solar system and space
	Ecology
	Conservation
	Simple machines

long the themes should take. The length of time the learners spend on each theme will affect how many themes fit into a school year.

Teachers plan for several curriculum cycles each year that represent rigorous curriculum that mesh Common Core State Standards. Teachers spend approximately 6–8 weeks to implement each topic. Planning for four or five cycles over a year is probably workable, allowing some flexibility in studying other themes that surface during the school year, if desired.

THEME WORKSHOP

In the MAC program, a regularly scheduled time each day may be set aside for *theme workshop*, which is integrated into a block schedule. For example, some multi-age schools teach a Discovery Workshop on Monday, Wednesday, and Friday from 9:30–11:50 a.m. In the block of time, a theme interdisciplinary workshop is team taught by teachers in the K–1, 2–3 classrooms. Each teacher of the team implements a theme lesson to one multi-age group of learners from 9:30–10:10 a.m. and then teaches the other multi-age group of learners the same lesson from 10:10–10:50 a.m.

This block schedule (see table 7.2) allows for flexibility of learners to be regrouped into other multi-age learning groups that might be different from the multi-age

Table 7.2. Sample Block Schedule

	Monday	Tuesday	Wednesday	Thursday	Friday
			Block Schedule for the Week		
8:00–8:50	Homeroom (grade needs addressed)	Homeroom (grade needs addressed)	Homeroom (grade needs addressed)	Homeroom (grade needs addressed)	Homeroom (grade needs addressed)
8:50–9:30	Reading workshop	Math Workshop	Reading Workshop	Math Workshop	Reading Workshop
9:30–10:10	Discovery Theme (Interdisciplinary Workshop)	Reading Workshop	Discovery Theme (Interdisciplinary Workshop)	Reading Workshop	Discovery Theme (Interdisciplinary Workshop)
10:10–10:50	Discovery Workshop continues	Orbital Studies	Discovery Workshop continues	Orbital Studies	Discovery Workshop continues
10:50–11:30	Writing Workshop	Writing Workshop	Writing Workshop	Writing Workshop	Reader's Theater
11:30–12:10	Lunch	Lunch	Lunch	Lunch	Lunch
12:10–12:50	Social Studies	Social Studies	Social Studies	Social Studies	Social Studies
12:50–1:30	Science	Science	Science	Science	Science
1:30–2:20	Learning Centers	Learning Centers	Learning Centers	Learning Centers	Learning Centers
2:10–2:50	Project-Based Learning Task	Project-Based Learning Task	Project-Based Learning Task	Project-Based Learning Task	Project-Based Learning Task

Note: Teachers will conduct small group work when needed.

homeroom. In another school, 40 minutes per day is called *theme time* and is scheduled for science and social studies. This theme time lesson is taught by one teacher
and each lesson is used for either introducing information, for research, for discussion, or for theme-related projects. No matter which schedule the MAC program
follows, a critical aspect of this theme teaching is to keep students interested and
engaged. Knowing when learners are not interested in the theme is a process that is a
key element to evaluate the potential success of the instruction being offered (Malloy,
Marinak, Gambrell, & Mazzoni, 2014).

The study of themes in *curriculum cycles* and the hands-on projects that grow out
of these studies provide teachers many ways to integrate active learning experiences
which are appropriate to each age group. In fact, there are advantages that accrue
from theme studies of curriculum cycles such as the following:

- Application of skills
- A variety of concrete experiences that allow learners to apply and understand
  concepts
- Social and leadership development inherent in teamwork and in learning from
  one another

INTERDISCIPLINARY TEACHING AND LEARNING

In MAC, theme studies are taught through an interdisciplinary model. Theme studies suggest the incorporation of one subject with others. An example of this is found
in themes that emphasize literacy across the discipline.

Interdisciplinary Studies Characteristics

Characteristics of interdisciplinary studies are the following:

- Interdisciplinary studies are organized in comprehensive plans that focus on a
  specific theme or problem.
- Interdisciplinary studies are explored by using the skills and techniques (ways of
  knowing content) associated with any academic discipline that can inform the
  theme or problem under investigation (Wood, 2010).
- Interdisciplinary studies place equal emphasis on the mastery of the content,
  concepts, skills, and processes involved in learning the theme or problem.
- Interdisciplinary studies accommodate student diversity by providing for the
  differentiation of the multi-age learner investigating and reporting information
  about the topic.
- Interdisciplinary approach is supported by findings from research on the human
  brain (Sousa & Tomlinson, 2011).

Human Brain and Multi-Age Learning

Brain research can be helpful when planning interdisciplinary studies for multi-age learners. Eric Jensen (2005) suggested that the brain makes associations and constructs meaning better when it finds patterns and relationships such as those that interdisciplinary methods provide. This approach is meaningful at all age levels because it helps students to note relationships among the various disciplines for the topics they study. This learning process is especially meaningful to older students because they may be more capable of detecting patterns due to their greater knowledgebase in the subject areas.

According to Costa and Kallick (2008), the brain makes associations and constructs meaning when participating in teaching strategies that are brain based for learning. The interdisciplinary model helps students to make these associations and acquire new learning. As Piaget (1985) mentioned, thematic study helps connect knowledge with experience and new ideas in terms of learners assimilating and accommodating new information.

Brain research supports the notion that a caring and safe learning environment encourages positive results for learning. Learning is more likely to occur when the brain is not threatened. This means that multi-age learners need to be willing to risk-take while making mistakes in a learning environment where they feel safe and will not be ridiculed when wrong. Such an environment encourages learners to reflect on what they know and do not understand.

When considering brain research and connecting *Habits of the Mind* (Costa & Kallick, 2008), the multi-age learner integrates a willingness to admit one's errors, stay open to new ideas, have an inquiry attitude, and be persistent at tasks. These are the elements of thinking that are necessary for multi-age learners to succeed and which are fostered through interdisciplinary studies (Costa & Kallick, 2008; Wood, 2010). Teachers are more interested in observing how students gain new knowledge rather than how they restate information.

Differentiation connects nicely to how the brain learns. There are seven basic principles that connect differentiation, brain research, and learning (Sousa & Tomlinson, 2011). Teachers in the MAC program are trained in these principles in order to respond to the diversity in the multi-age classroom:

- Each brain is unique. Each learner has individual preferences for learning and therefore curricular frameworks, instructional practices, and assessment tasks are different for all learners. The interdisciplinary approach allows students to work on different topics and at different levels based on the study of a theme.
- The brain often can retain more knowledge if it is retained in long-term memory. To do this, the frontal lobe is capable of looking for patterns and relationships that form new knowledge for the learner. The interdisciplinary model allows the learner to make connections across subject areas.
- It is important that teachers investigate ways to help multi-age learners apply divergent thinking. The frontal lobe is responsible for processing higher-order

thinking and solving problems creatively. This process encourages new ideas and expands cognitive networks in the brain. The learner is a problem solver during interdisciplinary tasks.

- The limbic system of the brain is where emotions are processed. When the brain produces positive chemicals in the learner, this process excites the learner and the multi-age student continues to explore learning opportunities. Targeting individual interests through differentiated experiences helps learners to focus more on gaining new information.
- Neurons fire in the brain when the learner experiences an emotion, but also when someone else experiences the emotion. Therefore, it is important that multi-age learners work in groups that are successful and as a result have constructive social interactions during learning. This process enhances learning and retention. The interdisciplinary unit allows students to work together to investigate problems about a theme and discuss new ideas that surface.
- The memory system of the brain carries information to the working memory which is temporary. Teachers are encouraged in the MAC program to use meaningful learning strategies—strategies that allow individuals to relate new knowledge to relevant concepts they already know. New knowledge must interact with the learner's knowledge structure of prior experiences if learning is to take place (Ausubel, 1968).
- Student's interest must be maintained if retention of new information is to take place. The brain is always searching for meaning. The MAC teacher tailors tasks to meet the individual needs of the multi-age learner while targeting the student's interest and focus during interdisciplinary studies.

Interdisciplinary studies units are brain friendly, interesting, and exciting. These units are implemented in collaborative classrooms where learners share ideas and acquire new knowledge based on an individual's prior experience. There are recommended practices in designing interdisciplinary units of study (Cozza, McDonough, & Laboranti, 2011; Wood, 2010, 2015).

1. Determine the topic, theme, or problem.
2. Write down the general objectives of the unit based on content knowledge, concepts, skills, and dispositions.
3. Identify the content learning standards to be met based on CCSS.
4. Generate some essential questions to guide the unit of study.
5. Design and record the unit assessment strategies.
6. Design the unit learning plan.
7. Use a unit web design to brainstorm unit ideas.
8. Write descriptions of lessons and tasks included in the web aligning objectives, standards, and assessment on the Lesson Planning Sheet.
9. List unit materials and resources needed.

What is the interdisciplinary approach to teaching and learning? It is an instructional framework that is student-centered and project-based—an approach designed to encourage students to see connections and to apply learning in one discipline to another discipline area (National Middle School Association, 2002; Vars, 1996). Students learn better if the subject matter can be generalized to other subjects and to their own concerns in the real world.

According to Fitzpatrick (1997), common components were created by the National Study of School Evaluation (NSSE) and the Alliance for Curriculum Reform (ACR) to encourage interdisciplinary teaching: problem-solving process skills, standards-based curriculum, communication skills, higher-level thinking processes, and cooperative learning. Research has stated that these components have been integrated into interdisciplinary studies for school improvement in school programs in three ways: teaming for promoting teacher collaboration across disciplines (Murata 2002); block scheduling; and interdisciplinary teaching by a self-contained teacher (Meister & Nolan, 2001).

Results have shown that students involved in an integrative curriculum do as well as, or better than, students in a departmentalized school program (National Association for Core Curriculum, 2000). A unit of study that uses the interdisciplinary approach in the lower grades enables teachers to differentiate instructional practices for each student and make links between disciplines. One goal for this approach is to give students a more relevant, less fragmented, and stimulating experience for learning (Hayes Jacobs, 1989, p. 10).

How Do Teachers Plan and Teach an Interdisciplinary Unit?

Steps to explore this approach are outlined by considering the topic selection, interdisciplinary questions, concept map, planning matrix, and lesson design and assessment strategies. The following ideas for developing a plan for the Interdisciplinary Unit Model (Cozza, McDonough, & Laboranti, 2011; Hayes Jacobs, 1989) are followed in MAC:

1. Choose a topic that is not too broad or too narrow that relates to the curriculum.
2. Brainstorm ideas by generating elements that may be answered by exploring the topic of study. During the brainstorm session all answers are important. The associations to the topic may include questions, topics, people, ideas, and any materials targeting the theme of study.
3. Construct a Bubble Concept Map—center the main topic in the middle bubble of the concept map and place subjects in bubbles around the topic to assist with framing ideas that connect subject areas to the topic. Working on a bubble concept map will reveal ideas that are interesting and that are not usually part of the curriculum.

4. Establish guiding questions and a scope and sequence to organize the development of the unit. The questions are related to the subject-area topics and Bubble Concept Map ideas. These questions provide an outline of the topics covered in the unit. These ideas give the sequence in which these topics are studied. The scope and sequence assists teachers in developing a time frame for how long the unit of study will be scheduled.

5. Developing a framework to outline the interdisciplinary unit is an effective planning tool that integrates topic, topic questions, lesson objectives, higher-level thinking processes, standards, teaching strategies, and assessments. Also, this tool assists with developing a curriculum map for week to week or month to month lesson planning and assessment. This planning framework aligns the assessment with the objectives for each lesson and gives a clear road map of how to operationalize the unit components.

6. Create a curriculum map to outline weekly or monthly plans. These curriculum maps are also good tools for planning short and long-term unit events.

7. Write and implement each lesson plan.

8. Implement Assessment Strategies in each lesson to review how effective the unit of study was for students. Some suggested formative assessment tools are the following: rubrics, checklists, project-based tasks, and journal writing.

9. Reflect on the unit topic through conversations with students considering the following prompts: What were the most interesting tasks of the unit? What were the most challenging situations? What did you enjoy about this unit of study? How might this unit be improved?

Generalizing the Interdisciplinary Approach

The following components should be considered when preparing for this type of instruction (Cozza, McDonough, & Laboranti 2011):

- Plan ahead and discuss the planning stage with students to gather important input.
- Decide on the purpose of the interdisciplinary connection—teaching with other teachers from different disciplines, block schedules, or self-contained classrooms.
- Select a topic that works for a grade-level topic in the curriculum.
- Construct a timeline.
- Integrate curriculum and interdisciplinary standards into unit objectives.
- Integrate cooperative learning, problem solving, discussion groups, projects, and whole class conversation time. Allow students to assist with constructing assessment tools.

Developing Interdisciplinary Theme Units: Strategies and Examples

When providing professional development to multi-age teacher teams, teachers begin by introducing how to organize curricular connections on a planning organizer. The planning organizer (see figure 7.1) allows teachers and administrators to think of a central theme and consider a variety of topics related to the central theme based on different subject areas.

Most subjects can contribute to the *theme of study* such as mathematics, reading, writing, science, social studies, and the arts. Not all subject areas need to be connected to every theme that is studied. One important connection is the field trip/ guest speaker/artifact web area. This theme connection allows the teacher team to connect outside studies, experiential experiences, speakers that share expertise on the topic, parent involvement, and any artifacts that connect to the topic.

How Is a Theme or Topic Selected and Planned?

In the MAC program, teachers use topics based on 3-year cycles. The themes in the program tend to be based on social studies and science themes, as mentioned in the beginning of this chapter. The following planning process often takes place during MAC PLC team meetings. First, the teachers identify a central theme, topic, or issue. For example, the teacher team for the Explorers (K–1) and Detectives (2–3) decided to study the topic of "sharks" because it was a theme in curriculum cycle 1 under "ocean life."

While these examples are planned with lower schoolchildren in mind, the techniques of interdisciplinary planning can be adapted also to upper levels of teaching and learning. The interdisciplinary planning web (see figure 7.1) can be a good guide to help teachers identify the various content domains that could be connected with the theme. Second, within each subject area, the teachers create a visual model of

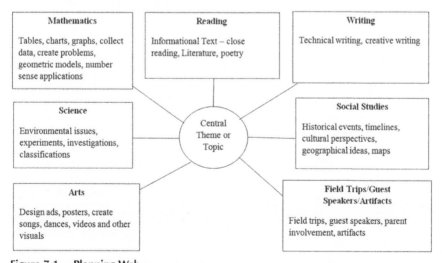

Figure 7.1. Planning Web
Source: Adapted from McDonald & Czernizk (1994).

the concepts that connect subject areas to the topic. Teachers generated a web on the topic of sharks (see figure 7.2) that connect related concepts considering Common Core State Standards and each subject domain.

Third, teachers connect the web ideas to a concept map that make the teaching and learning process meaningful for teachers and students. The concept maps allow teachers to visualize just how to connect different subject domains into a central theme that integrates tasks, concepts, and process skills into a unit plan. The concept map ideas in figure 7.3 depict a partial concept map on the topic of "sharks" in the ocean environment that teachers generated during the planning cycle with the multi-age learners.

Finally, the teachers develop specific lesson ideas on a planning sheet. These ideas integrate the topic, length of time for the study, subject areas and questions to guide lessons, resources needed, learning center ideas, and strategies to assess the learning processes. These components on the planning sheet connect to the web and concept map. For example, the teachers begin to generate the unit's essential questions using ideas from the concept map to guide the interdisciplinary plan. Some essential questions are: How are sharks classified? What type of habitats do sharks live? How do sharks impact the food chain? These essential questions drive the unit of study.

Next the teachers connect Common Core State Standards of three years, to make sure the needs of learners are accommodated with appropriate standard. Lessons objectives, tasks, and assessments are recorded on the plan sheet to make sure that accurate concepts are included in the lesson plan process.

Tasks are fun. In a mathematics lesson, students work in small groups and collect data about a shark: size, type, number of fins, and the like. Each group makes a life-size outline of the shark on butcher paper based on the data. In a science lesson, students work with partners to classify benthic (passive bottom sharks in

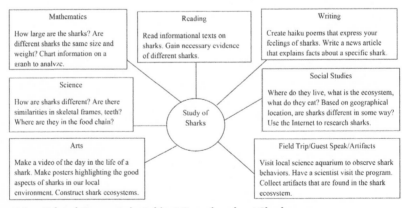

Figure 7.2.   Related Concepts in Subject Domains about Sharks
Source: Adapted from McDonald & Czernizk (1994).

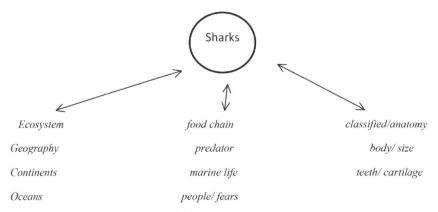

Figure 7.3.   Concept Map of Shark Ideas

shallow water) and oceanic (deep water) sharks. Each partnership is required to make a classification book of the different sharks and discuss the similarities and differences.

In a social studies lesson small groups research the habitats of sharks and then list habitat needs of the type of shark and construct a diorama of the shark and the habitat. Each student designs a "Save the Shark" poster by using pictures and sayings that integrate scientifically accurate information. The posters are displayed in the main gallery of the school building for the school community to view. In reading workshop, students read informational text to gain evidence of the different kinds of sharks. Each student constructs an informational booklet on the evidence.

Authors create haiku poems of five lines describing emotion and ideas about sharks in our world. Students write letters to Sea World, if an aquarium in the local area is not available. A guest speaker from a museum or aquarium visits the school to give a presentation on the shark environment. Parents receive a letter that asks them to collect artifacts that represent shark ideas such as URLs, software products, apps, photographs, published papers, and so on. Then parents visit the classrooms to present the artifacts that they were able to find.

PLANNING INTERDISCIPLINARY CURRICULUM IN THE MAC PROGRAM— LONG TERM, SHORT TERM

Long-term planning is critical in the MAC classrooms since you will teach the same children for several years rather than teach a different group each year. Based on planning for three years, a multi-age teacher can proceed to plan several themes. For example, in the Pandas (K–1) classroom, the learners may study animals in the local environment in the first year, build on the knowledge gained from the unit and select a theme of animals found in tropical areas the second year, and study animals in the polar regions the third year.

The 5-year-old children (kindergarten age) and 6-year-old children (first grade age) may study animals in the environment in the first year; the second year, kindergarten students as first graders continue to build on animals in the tropical areas; but the third year, the K–1 students have moved on and the new group that already studied animals in tropical area, will study animals in the polar regions the third year. Then, the teacher repeats the cycles once again with the new students in the multi-age classroom. This planning cycle is recorded on a Long-Term Planning Sheet to document teacher's planning ideas for the 3-year period (see table 7.3).

MAC Students Take Ownership to Theme Learning

The MAC program encourages that teachers hold planning sessions a variety of times during the year. This reflective planning process helps teachers to understand just how to move ahead with themes in the MAC program and work out just which class groups will collaborate on units of study. Children are part of the planning so that they take ownership to the learning processes. Webbing and K-W-L-H Charts are excellent strategies to address just what students know about a topic, prior to beginning the unit of study.

If you engage students in these brainstorm strategies, teachers will be able to identify how to approach lessons. For example, if students already have knowledge about the animals in the local environment, it would be helpful for the teacher to integrate animals found in the United States and compare the animals to the local environ-

Table 7.3.   Long-Term Planning Cycle Sheet

Year 1	Year 2	Year 3
Topics or themes **Animals in the Local Environment**	**Topic or themes** **Animals in the Tropical Areas**	**Topics or themes** **Animals in the Polar Regions**
Length of time of study	Length of time of study	Length of time of study
Subject areas and questions to guide the lessons	Subject areas and questions to guide the lessons	Subject areas and questions to guide the lessons
Resources needed	Resources needed	Resources needed
Centers	Centers	Centers
Projects	Projects	Projects
Learning tasks	Learning tasks	Learning tasks

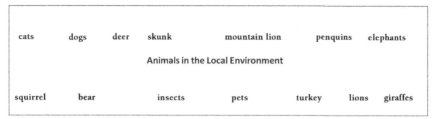

Figure 7.4. Brainstorm Session

ment. These brainstorming strategies also allow students to become interested and curious about the unit of study that will take place.

Brainstorm webbing is an excellent way to generate theme ideas based on the learners' interests and encourage curiosities of learners. For example, a teacher begins a theme of "Animals in the Local Environment" by placing the theme in the center of the Smart Board or chart paper. Children are asked to generate any ideas that come to mind about the topic. The teacher adds ideas and then decides on how to generate questions that they would like to answer. Children brainstorm ideas about *animals in the local environment* based on their prior experiences (see figure 7.4).

Some ideas are appropriate and other ideas are not. The teacher is the final authority on what will work based on good ideas and the resources that are available. The K-W-L-H Chart (see table 7.4) is a way to address a theme to find out what learners know (K), want to know (W), what they have learned (L), and how (H) they can learn more about the topic during their studies.

A K-W-L-H Chart is posted in the classroom so that learners can continue to add questions and information as they explore the theme. At the end of the study, learners will complete the L section on what they learned and H section of how they can learn more about the topic. Learners are encouraged to use their experiential knowledge from projects, field trips, guest speaker sessions, and learning centers to answer their own questions.

SNAPSHOT OF AN INTERDISCIPLINARY UNIT ON NATIVE AMERICANS

The Native American theme in the classroom of the Explorers (2–3) included reading, telling, and writing stories based on Native American legends. Mary Kay, the teacher, integrated art and social studies lessons with emphasis on observing pottery, Native American dresses, and weaving artifacts from pictures and Internet sites. Ethan, an 8-year-old, said, "I am having so much fun looking at all these artifacts from Native Americans. It's cool!" A field trip to the Museum of Natural History allowed young learners to see samples of these artifacts up close. In art class students created their own pottery and weaving with paper. In social studies class, learners dressed up with Native American garb and compared clothing of the Native Americans with their own clothing.

The children really enjoyed the dress-up sessions and they asked if they could create a parade around the multi-age corridors so all students could see the clothing. The children also studied music and dance, both traditional and invented to connect to the special and kinesthetic experiences of the learners. Mathematics was even connected with observations. The children looked for the geometric patterns of Native American designs and connected geometry concepts with the designs. Many of the students decided to make art posters that integrated the geometric patterns.

Table 7.4.   KWLH

K *What Do You Know?*	W *What Do You Want to Know?*	L *What Did You Learn?*	H *How Can You Learn More?*

It is important to note that in a multi-age classroom a variety of projects are going on at the same time and there are tasks for all learners at all levels. Learners can work alone, in heterogeneous groups, or with a partner, based on interests. These classrooms generate excitement during learning.

Project-Based Learning

PBL in the MAC program is an integral part of learning because it assists multi-age learners to select an assignment of interest and connect ideas to real-world problems that can connect to community and global issues. PBL is defined by many educators (Barell, 2010; Bender, 2012; Cole & Washburn-Moses, 2010; Larmer & Merendoller, 2010) as an effective way to engage students with their learning of content, concepts, and skills.

Students use authentic, real-world projects, based on an engaging question, task, or problem, to learn about interdisciplinary academic content and skills in a problem-based collaborative setting (Maloney, 2010). This environment encourages high-level thinking and increases achievement. As a result of the effective manner for learning, PBL is considered as a 21st-century teaching technique (Cole & Washburn-Moses, 2010).

In the MAC program, PBL is used on all levels of the multi-age classrooms to make connections to curricula, engage learners in exciting and independent learning situations, and encourage high-level thinking while targeting individual needs of each learner. PBL can be focused on one subject or might be targeting interdisciplinary concepts. We consider the following characteristics of PBL when planning tasks based on common features from research (Barell, 2010; Larmar & Mergendoller, 2010):

- *Anchor.* Present an introduction and background knowledge to set the stage and generate interest.
- *Collaborative Work.* Collaborative teamwork is important because it is a way to make learning experiences more authentic. In the MAC program, students are able to share their expertise with younger and older students.
- *PBL Question.* The question should engage students and focus their efforts based on their interests.
- *Feedback and Reflection.* Scaffold assistance should be ongoing and is always provided by the teacher and peers. This is a good opportunity for older children to assist younger children in the multi-age setting.
- *Inquiry and Innovation.* Learners are asked to use the broad question and generate additional questions focused more specifically on project tasks.
- *Reflection.* All learners are encouraged to reflect on projects during the PBL process.
- *Artifact or Product.* The group uses guidelines for project completion and artifact or product generation.
- *PBL Presented Publicly.* Projects are authentic answers to problems that are confronted in the real world. A public presentation of project is required.
- *Student Voice and Choice.* Learners have a voice in how the project might be undertaken. They must follow guidelines but they are encouraged to exercise choices throughout the project process.

How Does PBL Fit into the MAC Curriculum?

PBL is used in the MAC curriculum by using PBL as an adjunct to a unit of study or to replace unit-based instruction entirely. As an adjunct to a unit of study the teacher uses the PBL assignment to assist multi-age learners to synthesize curriculum standards at the end of the unit or as a problem explored throughout the unit study to enhance the learning process of the topic (Barell, 2010; Bender, 2012; Larmer & Mergendoller, 2010).

Standards are taught exclusively through the PBL experience and these standards are addressed in some way in the project process. In the MAC program we find advantages to PBL in MAC: teachers work in teams and collaborate on how PBL can be applied to the multi-age curriculum. Some teachers have more experience with this PBL process and therefore share their expertise with less experienced teachers.

Teaching partners and the teacher leaders in the school assist others through this process. In fact, some teachers may choose to replace their typical instructional unit with a PBL experience that they design with other teachers. This PBL teaching process also allows teachers to serve as facilitator as students move through their project tasks. This facilitator role is encouraged throughout the teaching process of MAC.

Research tells us the PBL agenda encourages deeper understanding of a topic by allowing students to gain an understanding of content and concepts increased with critical-thinking processes (Strobel & van Barneveld, 2008). This PBL process also enhances retention of information (Geier et al., 2008) and the process uses effective problem-solving strategies in academic areas (Strobel & van Barneveld, 2008).

PBL is effective with lower-achieving students because it helps to differentiate instruction for struggling students (Geier et al., 2008) and ELLs. Proponents of PBL recommend that students use cooperative group work because collaborative tasks echo the types of demands of the 21st-century career readiness environments. Working on an individual PBL is not as effective as problem solving and sharing ideas with other peers (Bender, 2012).

Description of PBL Tasks Components and Rubric

The following steps are followed during a PBL teaching and learning experience:

- Identify a topic.
- Select critical questions and problems.
- Brainstorm a solution to questions or problems.
- Work collaboratively with other students.
- Ask questions about the work of other students in the group.
- Determine the overall value of contributions of members of the PBL collaborative group.
- Develop or construct an artifact or product that communicates and culminates the results of the PBL project.

These PBL components are ideas for teachers and learners to consider for many new and innovative instructional duties and skills. It is important to realize that the role of teacher in a PBL process is *teacher facilitator* that assists with directing student groups to focus on appropriate resources for the project, answer questions through a brainstorming process, encourage students to work collaboratively with group members, and direct learners to reflect ongoing on the work of the PBL collaborative group.

Students in PBL groups are inquiring, investigating, questioning, and synthesizing information to answer critical questions and problems based on a topic. These are high-level skills that are necessary for a learner to use in order to be an independent learner in the 21st century. To differentiate instruction with that project, the teacher creates a heterogeneous group for differentiated tasks with each group. For example, a teacher selects a strong reader, a strong writer, a technology-savvy student, a student leader, and a share person for the group, and a student that is not too strong in reading, and the learners are asked to keep track of their responsibilities on a Project Responsibilities Recording Sheet (see table 7.5).

A rubric is used to evaluate each student and groups' performance (see table 7.6). Each student and group is evaluated using the Likert Scale Rubric. A 5 indicates excellent or couldn't be done any better, and a 1 indicates needs considerable improvement.

SNAPSHOT OF PBL IN MAC

Mr. Gates, the teacher of the Investigators (grades 4–5) class, presents a PBL assignment to students. These learners are asked to present a one-hour assembly to all multi-age classrooms to celebrate the coming of spring by studying the lifecycle of a plant. Various PBL groups are organized. Mr. Gates selects each student for an appropriate role: reader, writer, technology organizer, leader, and share person.

The PBL question is the following: How do plants grow? How can we present the life cycle of a plant and the importance of the changes that take place in the environment during the spring season? One student group decides that each group member needs to identify and describe the stages of plant life, define the plant life stages, obtain pictures showing the stages. Students research information on plant cycles, draw diagrams, create a video and PowerPoint, and find websites that give specific information.

Students set up plant experiments that include germination bags of seeds, recording the growth of a plant and analyzing the data. The artifacts that are anticipated are the following: writing a one-page report of each stage of the plant's life cycle, and integrate diagrams, pictures, and video showing stages of the plant cycle. Also, the PBL group is expected to organize a presentation including PowerPoint presentation and a video presentation summarizing the stages of plant life. Each student works through jobs that they feel they can complete. At the end of the three-week study, the PBL group presents to the school environment during a spring assembly.

Table 7.5. Project Responsibilities for PBL Group

Group Artifacts or Projects	Draft Date: Details on Status of Project	Final Date Artifact of Project Is Due; and Who Will Present the Artifact or Project	How Is the PBL Group Evaluated?

Table 7.6.   Rubric for PBL Artifact or Projects

Student or PBL Group Name _____ Date _____
Name of the PBL Assignment _____

Item	1	2	3	4	5
Researched the topic completely					
Presented numerous research resources					
Presented summaries of the information collected					
Synthesized information collected appropriately					
Presented the work in the most appropriate formats					
Overall evaluation of this project					

LEARNING CENTERS

Learning centers in the MAC program add to lessons in a variety of ways. Learning centers are different from stations in the classroom. Stations work in concert with one another. Students must move to each station to add to curricula understandings. Learning centers reteach, reinforce, and enrich curriculum concepts. Each learning center is distinct. Learning centers are used to differentiate instruction in a multi-age learning environment. Learning centers are located in various spots in the classroom. Learners are put into small groups or work in isolation and are given a task to accomplish in an allotted amount of time. Once the group (or learner) completes the task they move to the next center.

The learning centers should connect to curriculum, concepts, and skills that are currently studied in the classroom. For example, in a mathematics measurement center, learners have opportunities to investigate different measurement concepts using hands-on tasks and materials. Once the teacher knows what to focus on then the teacher determines how many centers will be needed. It is important to consider the following when setting up learning centers (Tomlinson, 2014):

- Focus on learning goals and standards.
- Contain materials that promote individual learning toward those goals.
- Use materials and tasks addressing a wide range of reading levels, learning abilities, and interests.
- Integrate tasks that vary from simple to complex, concrete to abstract, structured to open-ended.
- Provide clear and simple directions for learners.
- Give instructions about what a learner should do if he or she needs help.
- Give instructions about what a student should do when the assignment is complete.
- Use a record system and assessment framework to monitor what students do at the center.

It is important to include all materials needed for each center task and place the center task and materials into folders or baskets. A list of rules and behavior expectations should be presented to the learners and then posted to a bulletin board. A sign for each center and an organization chart to keep track of learners' completion of centers should also be available. These Learning Centers can be changed based on the need of the learners.

SNAPSHOT OF MULTI-AGE CLASSROOM LEARNING CENTER TIME

Teachers in a multi-age team often integrate learning centers into the current thematic unit. For example, if the theme of study is "animals in the tropical areas," the centers reflect this theme. In the Writing Center, learners write an informational text about animals in the tropics using a variety of reference books. In the Science Center, the children examine animal tracks and place them into categories. In the Art area, children paint pictures of animals considering the characteristics of the animal (color, shape, and size) and where they live. In the Mathematics Center, learners use data based on size of the animal and chart the height and weight of animals on a graph to compare and contrast different animals.

INDEPENDENT LEARNING—ORBITAL STUDIES

Orbital studies are independent investigations that happen in and out of the classroom. The orbital study's purpose is to allow a learner to work independently on a topic that is interesting for the student and is related to some facet of the curriculum. The study takes place for approximately three to six weeks, but length of time for the project will vary with student readiness, interest, and levels of learning (Tomlinson, 1999). A teacher guides students to develop an orbital study topic and questions, develop a plan for research, find resources, suggest ways to create a product or artifact to synthesize the topic of study, create a method of presentation, and design criteria for assessing the project. Teachers in the MAC program create Orbital Studies Research Packets for learners.

These packets have documents to guide learners through the investigation. The packet includes: a topic page with an area to generate questions to guide study, a space to list the purpose of the study, the reason why the learner selected the topic, and what information the learner wants to gain at the end of the project. A learner must keep a log of activities that were conducted on the investigation, and keep a journal reflection on each task that is completed. The learner must decide on the type of product that will be completed to show how content and concepts of the topic have been applied.

The learner must conference with the teacher once per week on the study project and share with at least three peers to gain feedback on the project. The final project and an oral presentation are conducted by the learner. The teacher gives a rubric to the learner to allow the learner to understand how the student is assessed on the final project. A teacher works with an individual student or a small group to help them select a topic and explain project components. A class teacher offers mini lessons to small groups of students on how to develop each Orbital Studies project component. All teachers assume responsibility for helping learners plan, research, and time-manage, and give feedback on an ongoing basis.

SNAPSHOT OF THE ORBITAL STUDIES

Dylan is 9 years old and is in the Voyager class (grades 4–5). He is building a space capsule that will travel to Mars. He is researching the types of rockets that can be used for the space voyage and connecting the solar system unit in class on investigating the planet of Mars. He uses the Internet to understand how long travel will be to reach the planet, what food will be needed for the voyage, how long the space travel will take, and what to expect when he lands on Mars.

He meets with Ms. Warner once per week to discuss his information that he has collected and how he will construct a Mars spacecraft. He has also started collecting Mars photographs found on the NASA site. He will use these photographs for his final presentation to his class. He uses his ongoing log sheet and reflective journal to show to Ms. Warner the activities he completes as he continues his Orbital Studies. He has been working on this project for two weeks and is making good progress. He continues to review the assessment rubric to assist him in understanding how he will be assessed once he completes the assignment.

Taisha is 7 years old and passionate about dance. She has decided to explore different dances in different cultures around the world. She is learning about countries around the world in "Discovery Workshop," an interdisciplinary unit that the Detectives class (grades 2–3) is presently studying. This connects with studies of geography and culture in social studies. She has found dances from different countries in Africa and Spain in the first week of her Orbital Studies. She plans to find the dances from four different geographical locations on the globe, describe how the dance connects to the culture, what music is used, and how dances are performed. She is hoping to write a description of each dance and actually perform one dance of her choice. She will present an oral reading and a dance performance for a final project.

Sophia is 6 years old in the Explorer class (grades K–1). She loves to play doctor and understand the human body. She listens to heart beats using a variety of devices. She looks at Internet sites to understand the human body parts. She has made a drawing of her own body by allowing her friend to take an outline of herself while she lies down on the large brown paper. She researches the heart, lungs, and stomach. She creates drawings of these parts and pastes them on her body image. She writes stories about each body part. She shares her ideas to the class as she completes each part.

Gabe is a 12-year-old in the Divers class (grades 6–8). He has read a variety of types of literature this year, including poetry. He has decided to explore a variety of poets and poems to look at how "metaphor" is integrated in poems. He plans to create a book on each poet and poem that he investigates.

DIFFERENTIATION, ENGLISH LANGUAGE LEARNERS, AND SPECIAL NEEDS LEARNERS

Orbital Studies allow differentiation of content because students select their own topics of interest, research materials, develop plans, and select from a wide range of options about how to culminate their learning through creating products or artifacts. The teacher monitors learners' progress and coaches each student to give appropriate individual instruction to target the needs of each learner. ELLs are able to use visuals to connect to concepts. Special needs learners integrate a variety of sensory materials to complete projects.

EDUCATOR'S REFLECTION

Curriculum cycles help MAC teachers to repeat themes every four years. This process eliminates the problem of repeating topics of study that students have already learned about in a previous year. Students benefit from learning through an interdisciplinary unit because it makes connections from subject to subject to make learning meaningful. This type of approach allows for students to generalize concepts to new situations and it encourages higher-level thinking processes.

Brain research supports interdisciplinary approach because students are able to make connections and generalize learning to real-world situations. The designer of the unit determines the scope and sequence, planning framework, and questions to avoid scattered sampling of activities that have no real meaning to the teaching and learning process. The guiding force to interdisciplinary planning and implementation is for effective teaching and learning.

APPLICATION OF CONCEPTS FOR ALL SCHOOL SYSTEMS

All school programs should encourage the following:

- Integrate interdisciplinary learning units to help students make connections across disciplines.

- Brain research suggests that learners should be involved in tasks that help them generalize learning to real-world situations.
- PBL, Learning Centers, and Orbital Studies are independent tasks that allow students to explore and investigate topics and think on high levels.

REFERENCES

Ausubel, D. (1968). *Educational psychology: A cognitive view*. New York, NY: Holt, Rinehart & Winston.

Barell, J. (2010). Problem-based learning: The foundation for 21st century skills. In J. Bellanca & R. Brandt (Eds.), *21st century skills: Rethinking how students learn*. Bloomington, IN: Solution Tree Press.

Bender, W. N. (2012). *Project-based learning: Differentiating instruction for the 21st century*. Thousand Oaks, CA: Corwin.

Cole, J. E., & Washburn-Moses, L. H. (2010). Going beyond "the math wars." A special educator's guide to understanding and assisting with inquiry-based teaching in mathematics. *Teaching Exceptional Children, 42*(4), 14–21.

Costa, A. L., & Kallick, B. (2008). Describing the habits of mind. In A. L. Costa & B. Kallick (Eds.), *Learning and leading habit of the mind*. Alexandria, VA: ASCD.

Cozza, B., McDonough, P., & Laboranti, C. (2011). *The Scarlet Letter* from a geometric perspective. *Kappa Delta Pi Record 47*(4), 181–186.

Fitzpatrick, K. A. (1997). *Indicators of schools of quality: Vol. 1, Schoolwide indicators of quality*. Schaumburg, IL: National Study of School Evaluation.

Geier, R., Blumenfeld, P. C., Marx, R. W., Krajcik, J. S., Fishman, B., Soloway, E., & Clay-Chambers, J. (2008). Standardized test outcomes for students engaged in inquiry-based science curricula in the context of urban reform. *Journal of Research in Science Teaching, 45*(8), 922–939. DOI: 10.1002/tea.20248

Hayes Jacobs, H. (1989). *Interdisciplinary curriculum: Design and implementation*. Alexandria, VA: ASCD.

Jensen, E. (2005). *Teaching with the brain in mind* (2nd ed.). Alexandria, VA: Association for Supervision and Curriculum Development.

Larmer, J., & Mergendoller, J. R. (2010). 7 Essentials for project-based learning. *Educational Leadership, 68*(1), 34–37.

Malloy, J., Marinak, B. A., Gambrell, L. B., & Mazzoni, S. A. (2014). Assessing motivation to read. *The Reading Teacher, 67*(4), 273–282.

Maloney, D. H. (2010). Solving problems that count. *Educational Leadership, 68*(1), 55–58.

McDonald, J., & Czernizk, C. (1994). Developing interdisciplinary units: Strategies and examples. *School Science and Mathematics, 94*(1), 5–10.

Meister, D. G., & J. Nolan Jr., J. (2001). Out on a limb on our own: Uncertainty and doubt in moving from subject-centered to interdisciplinary teaching. *Teachers College Record, 103*(4), 608–633.

Murata, R. (2002). What does team teaching mean? A case study of interdisciplinary learning. *Journal of Educational Research, 96*(2), 67–77.

National Association for Core Curriculum. (2000). *A bibliography of research in the effectiveness of block-time, core, and interdisciplinary team teaching programs*. Kent, OH: NACC.

National Middle School Association. (2002). *Position statement on curriculum integration.* Westerville, OH: NMSA.

Piaget, J. (1985). *The equilibration of cognitive structures.* Chicago, IL: University of Chicago Press.

Sousa, D. A., & Tomlinson, C. A. (2011). *Differentiation and the brain: How neuroscience supports the learner-friendly classroom.* Bloomington, IN: Solution Tree Press.

Strobel, J., & van Barneveld, A. (2008). When is PBL more effective? A meta-synthesis of meta-analyses comparing PBL to conventional classrooms. *Interdisciplinary Journal of Problem-based Learning, 3*(1), 44–58.

Tomlinson, C. A. (1999). *The differentiated classroom: Responding to the needs of all learners.* Alexandria, VA: Association for Supervision and Curriculum Development.

Tomlinson, C. A. (2014). *The differentiated classroom: Responding to the needs of all learners* (2nd ed.). Alexandria, VA: ASCD.

Vars, G. F. (1996). Effects of interdisciplinary curriculum and instruction. In P. S. Hiebowitsh & W. G. Wraga (Eds.), *Annual review of research for school leaders* (pp. 147–164). Reston, VA: National Association of Secondary School Principals and Scholastic Publishing.

Woods, K. E. (2010). *Interdisciplinary instruction for all learners K–8: A practical guide.* New York, NY: Pearson.

Wood, K. E. (2015). *Interdisciplinary Instruction: Unit and lesson planning strategies K–8.* Long Grove, IL: Waveland Press.

IV

ASSESSMENTS AND SYSTEMIC CHANGE

8

Classroom Assessment in the Multi-Age Classroom

Ms. Lagoon is a teacher for the Anthropologists (grades 4–5). She teaches in a multi-age school that focuses on Cultures in the World. She realizes that class assessment is much more than creating and scoring paper-and-pencil tests. She finds that since she has taken over a multi-age classroom, she needs help deciding on just how to assess students' performance in reading, writing, math, and interdisciplinary tasks. Orbital studies and PBL events lack a specific assessment tool. She asks her teacher leader to give her advice. Marian, the teacher leader for the upper school, gives her some formative assessment ideas that focus on curriculum goals. However, Ms. Lagoon asks for specific examples that she can use in the classroom.

This chapter discusses specific examples that multi-age teachers often use when tracking the progress of each individual learner on an ongoing basis. All teachers in the MAC program assess learners through formative tasks while observing students, tracking learners' content understandings, and encouraging students to reflect on learning. Although summative assessments are used in the MAC school programs, in this chapter we are only focusing on some formative assessment strategies.

FORMATIVE ASSESSMENT STRATEGIES FOR MULTI-AGE LEARNING

Teachers often question the differences between formative and summative assessments. Formative assessments are assessments for learning and summative assessments are assessments of learning (Stiggins, Arter, Chappuis, & Chappuis, 2004). The question that surfaces from many educators is the following: What makes an assessment formative? According to DuFour, DuFour, Eaker, and Many (2010a) there are three important issues that occur for the assessment to be formative: the assessment is used to identify students who are experiencing difficulty, students are provided additional time and support to acquire the intended objective, and learners are given the opportunity to demonstrate that they have learned the concepts and skills.

Formative assessment is used to advance student's learning; assessment informs the teacher regarding the effectiveness of instruction and allows the learner to make progress at a proficient level (DuFour, DuFour, Eaker, & Many, 2010b). The format of the assessment tool is not important; rather it is the reason for using the tool (Tomlinson & Moon, 2013).

When working with differentiated learning environments, as in multi-age classrooms, learners have time to practice and make errors. They are given time to learn and understand the concepts before having a test or another form of evaluation (Tomlinson & Moon, 2013). The tool is a summative assessment if for some reason assessment occurs after the learning is complete and a grade is provided as a final measure to the learner's performance results.

In MAC PLCs and multi-age classrooms, teachers work collectively on how to break down a Common Core Standard. The standard defines the knowledge and skills students should have within their education careers so that they will graduate high school able to succeed in entry-level college and workforce programs (Common Core State Standards Initiative, 2010).

A formative assessment tool is written around the standards and learning targets (specific skills and strategies) integrated in a lesson. The learning target is important because it is the step-by-step processes that we use to teach the multi-age learners as they move to understanding the bigger concept.

The learning target allows students to know what they are aiming to understand in a lesson, what they need to do to have success, and what it looks like when they hit their learning target. Teachers in the MAC program verbally share this information with their students prior to each lesson. Their language is always very descriptive, specific, developmentally appropriate, and student friendly (Moss & Brookhart, 2012).

Some prompts from the teacher:

- "We are learning to . . ."
- "We show that we can do this by . . ."
- "We will look for evidence so that we know we are learning this by . . ."
- "It is important to understand this because . . ."

The teachers use an I-Can framework such as in the upper school:

- "I can learn to create an effective paragraph in my story to persuade our audience what we want them to agree with."

In the lower school:

- "We are learning to find action verbs in a story. We will know we can do this when we are able to say: I can read a story and circle all the action verbs I find" (Moss & Brookhart, 2012).

To assess the aim of the lesson, students often work in pairs. Learners are given a rubric that includes a rating scale of 1 to 3 (3 the highest score for performance and 1 the lowest score for performance). Students sit with a partner and take turns completing the rubric and self-assess their performance of the lesson. The rubric asks the following three statements:

- I can look for action verbs in a story.
- I can find evidence in the story.
- Now I can use these action verbs in my own stories.

The *unwrapping process* of the lesson's learning target assists our teachers to write formative assessments that align with lesson objectives. For example, the unwrapping process for the learning targets on "main idea" is the following: determine the main idea of the passage → differentiate between main idea and details → review the details → explain how details support the main idea (Bailey & Jakicic, 2012).

It is important to assess the processes that we teach learners so that teachers can identify and respond to learners who need more help with the learning targets. Learners that understand the lesson concepts move on to a new lesson. In the MAC program, fluid grouping of teaching concepts to students at different learning target levels accommodates the needs of learners.

CLASSROOM ASSESSMENTS

In MAC, teachers are encouraged to use a variety of formative assessment strategies ongoing to gather immediate feedback during a lesson. These assessments help the teacher determine if the learner knows or does not know the concept that is taught. Quality formative assessments include the following elements:

- Check for understanding using questions.
- Monitor learners as they work (in groups or independently) to give support when needed.
- Use individual white boards to record ideas.
- Integrate exit slips that ask a few questions about the lesson.
- Journal to reflect on the lesson ideas.
- Conduct a debriefing session to share what each group or a student learned in the lesson and conduct conferences.
- Integrate projects that connect to the learning targets of the lesson.

Examples of Classroom Assessments

Rubrics

In an all-inclusive manner, holistic rubrics are formative assessment tools that review just how a student performs on a specific task. The scale for grading in the

MAC program is often not based on a numerical value. The scale for grading is presented in a way that is positive so that students realize that they should continue to work the best way possible. In table 8.1 the Holistic Rubric scale for grading uses positive words and phrases such as *Wow! Great Ideas, Right-on—You are doing a great job! Moving-along—watch for details, Not yet.* This type of assessment is included in a family community that is caring and understanding of the student (see table 8.1).

Analytical rubrics are assessment tools that review different levels of learning for the student. An analytic rubric resembles a grid with the criteria for a student product listed in the left column and with levels of performance listed across the top row. These rubrics often use numbers or descriptive titles. The cells within the center of the rubric may be left blank or may contain descriptions of what the specified criteria look like for each level of performance (Jackson, 2017).

When scoring with an analytic rubric each of the criteria is scored individually. The following example in table 8.2 is used by teachers in a multi-age classroom for reading. It is used frequently in the lower school because it makes assessment quick and manageable. The results of the use of the rubric give enough information of how a student is performing.

For example, the teacher listens to students in a guided reading group to assess punctuation, fluency, comprehension, and vocabulary. Each student reads to the teacher and the teacher uses an analytical rubric to score the performance of the learner by circling each criterion for the student's level of performance on the task.

Checklists

Checklists in the multi-age program are used frequently because teachers tend to observe often and record learners' learning performances. Checklists can be a developmental assessment tool that reviews a student's performance in mathematics content strands for the school year. The content strand is listed and then the teacher takes notes from class observations of a student. The notes are recorded under the

Table 8.1.   Holistic Rubric/General

Scale for Grading	Description
Wow! Great Ideas.	Goes far beyond assignment; gives greater detail; includes additional information; is innovative
Right-on. You are doing a great job!	Completes task appropriately; shows understanding; meets requirements; is accurate
Moving along—watch for details.	Shows understanding but makes errors or is inconsistent; addresses task but may use inappropriate procedures; work lacks polish or is missing details; work reveals that understanding is in progress
Not yet.	Lacks understanding; does not address task; needs help or intervention

Table 8.2.   Analytic Rubric

Category	1	2	3
Punctuation	Does not understand punctuation in sentences	Uses punctuation some of the time	Has a good grasp of punctuation
Fluency	Does not read with speed, accuracy, and proper expression	Reads some of the time with speed, accuracy, and proper expression	Fluent reader that reads smooth with expression and adds intonation appropriately
Comprehension	Does not understand the passage	Understands the passage based on the concept sometimes	Is able to select evidence to support answers
Vocabulary	Does not understand numerous words	Understands some of the vocabulary using text to help	Has a good understanding of vocabulary words using evidence

specific month of the assessment. This type of mathematic developmental checklist (see figure 8.1) is an overview of student's performance for a year-long program.

The Reading Weekly Checklist is also used to record observations in the classroom. This weekly checklist can record student's accomplishments in reading for the week based on the reading concepts taught throughout the five days. The Reading Weekly Checklist (see figure 8.2) can include a rating scale of 1 through 5 to give a quantitative measure that can be used for the report card evaluation system, if need be.

An ideal strategy is to create an observation notebook through the use of a folder and index cards. This folder allows for teachers to easily organize assessments for multiple multi-age classes. Many teachers find this strategy to work during an interdisciplinary theme workshop, orbital studies, project-based tasks, and learning centers. Students move in and out of a variety of classrooms and tasks with different teachers presenting a variety of workshops. Teachers find this tool to help keep assessment manageable. The way it is set up is the following:

- A standard manila file folder is used for each multi-age class.
- The teacher needs an index card 5" x 7" for each student.
- The teacher opens the file folder and beginning at the bottom of the folder tapes each index card above the next, leaving about 1/2 inch on which to write each student's name.
- By taping the card on each side of the folder, the teacher flips the cards up to write on the card below it.
- The objectives of the lesson that are assessed are written on each card.

Ages 5-10

Name of Student _____

Date: _____

Content Strands	Sept.	Oct.	Nov.	Dec.	Jan.	Feb.	Mar.	April	May

Figure 8.1.   Mathematics Development Checklist

- The teacher moves through the classroom to record anecdotal ideas about how each student is targeting the objectives of the lesson.

Learning Logs and Student Engagement

Reflective learning logs are used to collect data on what students do when solving problems. Students are asked to write the problem of the lesson in the log. Then, the learner is asked to record what the problem is asking, what steps can be followed to solve the problem, what the student knows, what the student needs to find out, and what were the results. The student ends the reflection in the log by explaining what was learned and justifies the solution.

Ages 5-10

Name of Student _____

Week: _____

Rating Scale: 1 (lowest) through 5 (highest)

Week of:									

Figure 8.2.   Reading Weekly Checklist

These logs become very meaningful for assessing the student because the teacher is able to review the student's responses and understand what exactly the student knows or does not understand. The student may use writing, drawings, diagrams, or other ways to explain solutions.

Teachers also use prompts as one technique that is useful for a student to reflect on learning. Learners are asked to reflect in their learning logs by responding to prompts such as:

- Today I learned . . .
- The most useful thing I will take from this lesson . . .
- I was very interested to find out . . .
- One thing I am not sure about is . . .
- I want to know more about . . .

Asking students to choose a few prompts to respond to after a lesson encourages students to be thoughtful about their learning and encourages metacognitive reflection or introspection.

Student Engagement in Group Work

Students work often with other students. Most of the time, students work in cooperative learning groups to complete tasks. One issue that often surfaces in the multi-age setting is that the high-achieving students work at a different speed and low achieving students move at a different pace. Teachers remind learners when students work together in a group that all students help each other to succeed. For example, in mathematics workshop, learners realize that they are to work as mathematicians do. It is not so important to get the right answer as it is to be able to communicate one's findings to other mathematicians (William, 2011).

Also, students should be communicating with students by sharing ideas to try to find the solution to the problem. To assess this group session, the group members need to decide on the findings and then explain how an answer was reached. Not only are students developing content understandings and skills, but these learners also develop how to communicate mathematically (William, 2011).

SNAPSHOT OF FORMATIVE ASSESSMENT TOOL

Mr. Dean, a teacher for the Rangers (grades 3–4), presents a mathematics problem to the class and uses group debriefing to assess what the students learned in the lesson. Students work in collaborative groups to find the answer to the following: The groups are given a square grid 8 x 6. The problem is that each floor tile is 1-foot square. The students must find the perimeter of the floor.

Groups worked for approximately 20 minutes to solve the problem. Then, each group recorded their solution on a whiteboard and shared with the class. Some groups found that the answer was 48 and only one group showed that if you count the squares around the floor you find the perimeter. Mr. Dean was so confused that students had a difficult time finding the perimeter.

After discussing the situation with other teachers at a PLC meeting, the teacher group came to the consensus that the students needed values placed on the grid. It was confusing to the learners because they really were not sure just how to find perimeter. As a result, Mr. Dean retaught the concept of perimeter in the next lesson.

This is a good example of how students work together to solve problems. This debriefing process often gives a good snapshot of what students are thinking. From this scenario, reteaching targets is just what learners need.

BENEFITS OF COMMON ASSESSMENTS IN MULTI-AGE LEARNING ENVIRONMENTS

In the MAC program, our teachers work in PLC teams. Our teams not only use classroom assessments on an ongoing basis, but they also engage in collective inquiry. Teachers build shared knowledge around best practices and they discuss how to improve student learning. One strategy they use is to write *common formative assessments* around learning targets the team has identified as the most important ones to be taught.

For example, in the school that has adopted literacy across the curriculum as a school theme, the staff has written in their vision plan that all learners in the school will be excellent writers. To meet this objective in the vision plan, PLC teams outline what types of writing will be used in all multi-age classrooms. In the Literacy Academy learners are expected to write narrative, expository, fiction, and poetry. The PLCs plan specific assignments and use common assessments to view the progress of learners.

These common assessments are student work samples, completed graphic organizers, writing samples, products/projects, or performances. The team writes a few learning targets and align assessments to the targets. DuFour et al. (2010b) define common assessments as a means to encourage collective responsibility by teachers.

Teachers use the same common assessments for group work. Teachers on the team create a rubric and practice collaborative scoring to assess the assignment in the same way (Bailey & Jakicic, 2012). Groups of learners are expected to acquire the same knowledge and skills on their level. These assessments evaluate how well the student understands concepts and skills. Teachers find that these common assessments do not take long to administer and these assessment tools are scored quickly. The team can respond right away if they identify that a learner is having difficulty with a learning target.

In addition, the team will respond to learners' needs by providing additional instruction and support through interventions that are timely, directive, and systematic (DuFour et al., 2010a). Teams that use *common formative assessments* have more in-depth discussions about proficiency and have more focused conversations about multi-age instructional practices (Graham & Ferriter, 2008).

Interventions may range on different levels such as: targeting fluid groups after a session, assessing after applying differentiated instructional strategies, and assessing during enrichment opportunities. For example, in the Literacy Academy PLC teams analyze student work on how to build the action of a character in the story.

Teams move multi-age learners from one classroom into another for a short period of time to provide specific and targeted learning support on how to build a character in a story based on the learner's needs. One teacher determines which group to work with based on students that need more time and support. Another teacher takes a group to provide additional practice, and the third teacher takes learners that can benefit from enrichment.

Teachers may not opt out of this assessment process because one of the program principles of PLCs in the MAC program is that teams engage in collective inquiry and learn together. We call this process corrective instruction because alternative instructional practices take place for learners whose assessment results show they need more help, build on what they know already, or expand on their learning.

What is important to understand in the MAC program is that this common assessment process is different than the initial instructional practices because teachers offer more instruction on what each multi-age learner needs.

PORTFOLIOS FOR MULTI-AGE LEARNING

In the MAC program, portfolio assessment is one of many methods of collecting student data about what students know or do not know in relation to instructional goals and objectives. It is good way for teachers, students, and parents to see an overall picture of each student's growth. It is important for each learner to understand his or her progress, rather than be judged with classmates.

A portfolio is not a random collection of student work. The content of the portfolio is defined in the MAC classrooms with two purposes: to show the learner's growth and hold a collection of early works of the learner (even if the samples are not the best work of the learner), and to show the best work of the student of which the student will be evaluated. The last part of any portfolio is the evaluation process.

A clear evaluation statement of the purpose of intent of the evaluation should be stated clearly. Our teachers are encouraged to use checklists, rubrics, a student-teacher conference sheet, and student self-reflection of samples.

Steps that students and teachers following for the portfolio evaluation process are the following:

- The teacher gives an instructional objective to the learners from multi-age classrooms of ages seven through twelve and asks learners if they can select a sample from the work that represents that they have met the lesson objective. Young children select work samples based on the direction of the teacher.
- Next, each student meets with the teacher to discuss the sample. If the teacher agrees with the student that the sample meets the criterion, then the student moves to the next step.
- The student writes a short reflection (see figure 8.3) of why the sample work was chosen and explains its value.
- We ask that the learner takes the portfolio sample home so that parents (see figure 8.3) can also comment on it.
- Then, the student places the sample in the portfolio and the teacher evaluates it.

EVALUATION OF THE PORTFOLIO

The evaluation of the portfolio must have a specific goal. For example, in an Anthropologists' (grades 4–5) multi-age classroom for mathematics, the portfolio goal for sample work is based on a standard for measurement. Once the goal is set and the sample work and reflections are recorded, the teacher evaluates the portfolio using the following Portfolio Rating Scale Checklist (see table 8.3). This

---

Name of Learner:
Portfolio Sample Work Goal:

Reflection Sheet for Portfolio

Why I think this sample work should be placed in my portfolio. I like this sample because

_____

This sample work shows that I learned _____

_____

Parents' Comments
This sample work shows that my child _____

Teacher's Comments
This sample work shows that the learner _____

Figure 8.3.   Portfolio Reflection Sheet

Table 8.3. Portfolio Rating Scale Checklist

Sample Work Goal

CCSS Standards

Descriptor	0–1	2	3	4	5	Notes
Learner applies academic vocabulary	Not mentioned or rarely integrated	A few words are mentioned but not used appropriately	Some words are used correctly	Numerous words and concepts are integrated in sample appropriately	Outstanding application	
Learner represents content understanding in subject discipline	Not mentioned or rarely integrated	A few ideas mentioned but not used appropriately	Some ideas are used correctly	Numerous ideas are integrated in sample appropriately	Outstanding application	
Learner applies concepts	Not mentioned or rarely integrated	A few ideas are mentioned but not used appropriately	Some ideas are used correctly	Numerous ideas are integrated in sample appropriately	Outstanding application	
Learner applies skills	Not mentioned or rarely integrated	A few skills are mentioned but not used appropriately	Some skills are used correctly	Numerous skills and are integrated in sample appropriately	Outstanding application	
Miscellaneous	Not mentioned or rarely integrated	Mentioned but not used appropriately	Some ideas used correctly	Numerous ideas are integrated in sample appropriately	Outstanding application	

rubric allows a teacher to quickly rate the student sample and make notes about the evaluation.

Once the portfolio sample is evaluated by the teacher, the sample is placed in the student portfolio. Students are allowed to review their portfolios to review the learning that has taken place. Older students are allowed to generate their own goals for the portfolio and integrate sample work to demonstrate such learning. It is important to keep the learner involved with the learning process through the use of a portfolio.

English Language Learners and Students with Special Needs

A portfolio system is important to ELLs, students with special needs, and different ability level learners because this assessment system provides motivation for students. Learners respect the fact that they have a portfolio that traces their progress in understanding content, concepts, and skills in the curriculum. It also allows learners to make choices on which samples should be saved in the portfolio. This portfolio process allows the teacher to see learners as individuals so that interventions and accommodations can be made, if necessary.

EDUCATOR'S REFLECTION

Managing an assessment whether using classroom formative assessments, common assessments or a portfolio system can be overwhelming to teachers. In the MAC program, teachers work in teams and support each other. They have ongoing dialogue about how to use the assessment process successfully for all students. All classroom assessments allow the learner to continue to reflect on what he or she knows and does not know. They also give ongoing feedback to teachers on each individual multi-age student and the progress of that student.

A class portfolio for each child should be set up early in the school year. This portfolio that holds a collection of formative assessments, allow the teacher to use these data when setting up fluid groups to target student needs, give data for reports and complete report card grading. Assess students before beginning to teach a topic or skill. Pre-assessments can be in very easy forms such as a few problems to solve, a journal response, or even a few questions to answer. Review the results of the pre-assessment and plan lessons to meet students' needs. Keep assessing students on all work such as discussions, group activity, journal entries, centers, orbital studies, and PBL products and use these assessments as indicators of student need, rather than just assign a grade for report card evaluations.

APPLICATION OF CONCEPTS FOR ALL SCHOOL SYSTEMS

All school programs should encourage the following:

- Allow a variety of formative assessments to integrate into all lessons.
- Give students opportunities to have their own voice in organizing assessments.
- Portfolios are excellent assessment systems to collect data on students over time. All classrooms should have them.

REFERENCES

Bailey, K., & Jakicic, C. (2012). *Common formative assessment: A toolkit for professional learning communities at work*. Bloomington, IN: Solution Tree Press.

Common Core State Standards Initative. (2010). Retrieved from http://www.corestandards.org

DuFour, R., DuFour, R., Eaker, R., & Many, T. (2010a). *Learning by doing: A handbook for professional learning communities at work* (2nd ed.). Bloomington, IN: Solution Tree Press.

DuFour, R., DuFour, R., Eaker, R., & Many, T. (2010b). Professional learning commit glossary of key terms and concept. Retrieved from www.allthingsplc.info/df/links/terms.pdf

Graham, P., & Ferriter, B. (2008). One step at a time. *Journal of Staff Development, 29*(3), 38–42.

Jackson, I. E. (2017). *Types of rubrics*. Chicago, IL: DePaul University Teaching Commons. Retrieved from http://resources.depaul.edu/teaching-commons/teaching-guides/feedback-grading/rubrics/Pages/types-of-rubrics.aspx

Moss, C. M., & Brookhart, S. M. (2012). *Learning targets: Helping students aim for understanding in today's lesson*. Alexandria, VA: ASCD.

Stiggins, R. J., Arter, J. A., Chappuis, J., & Chappuis, S. (2004). *Classroom assessment for student learning; Doing it right—using it well*. Portland, OR: Assessment Training Institute.

Tomlinson, C. A., & Moon, T. R. (2013). *Assessment and student success in a differentiated classroom*. Alexandria, VA: ASCD.

William, D. (2011). *Embedded formative assessment*. Bloomington, IN: Solution Tree Press.

9

Improving the Program with Evidence from Practice

Just into six months of implementing the multi-age program, the Discovery School staff members were feeling that they needed to have feedback on how successful or unsuccessful the program was moving along. The staff decided that reflecting on the PLC process and creating instructional rounds and lesson study would be just the way to collect data. The teachers and leaders of the school decided to create a PLC rubric to assess how a PLC meeting discussion targets the needs of the program. PLC rubric questions focused on assessing the roles of the team, reflecting on member's participation, sharing of each member's expertise, applying professionalism during discussions, and targeting appropriate goals.

This staff started to put together instructional rounds by asking teachers, leaders, coaches, and consultants to join an instructional rounds research group. This research group decided to schedule one hour blocks, at least three times per year. Their role would be to move through classrooms and conduct instructional rounds in each classroom. Each round would be connected to the problems of practice that was generated by the classroom teachers and leaders.

After each session, the research group is responsible for debriefing about which behaviors were observed in each classroom. During the debrief session, charts are posted on walls and labeled successes or challenges. The "problem of practice" is always listed above the labeled columns. Evidence recorded on sticky notes is posted on the chart under each classroom teacher's name. The evidence generates an in-depth discussion by participants in the debrief session.

It was also decided by the school staff that "lesson study" would be scheduled twice per year. This lesson study process allows teachers to collaborate on creating a model lesson. One teacher volunteers to implement the lesson, while the research group observes what students are doing, during the lesson. After the lesson, a follow-up debrief session takes place. Teachers and the research group discuss the successes and ways to improve the lesson.

The MAC program has a strong agenda for integrating shared leadership strategies for reforming schools. As defined in chapter 1, the leaders, teachers, and other collaborators use PLCs, instructional rounds, and the lesson study process to collect evidence from practice to improve the program effectiveness.

EVIDENCE FROM PRACTICE—
PLCS, INSTRUCTIONAL ROUNDS, LESSON STUDY

The next few sections of this chapter will provide a detailed account of how educators typically practice MAC PLCs, instructional rounds, and lesson study. Sample evidence for each improvement strategy is presented.

MAC PLC Evidence

In a multi-age program, MAC PLC members collaborate to plan lessons, develop formative assessments, and discuss just how to build on successes and improve areas that need attention. The following discussion depicts how evidence is collected in a collaborative way.

All reflective strategies are formulated based on the *problem of practice*, and each strategy integrates this problem to guide the process. As described in detail in chapter 1, the problem of practice is defined as focusing on an instructional problem based on data or a problem that is observable in the classroom (Roberts, 2012).

In the MAC program, it is encouraged that the school staff create a working log folder prior to collecting any evidence during a PLC meeting, instructional round session, or lesson study. In the log folder the materials include the following: the day's problem of practice with the focus questions for the session, PLC data information, instructional rounds, and lesson study observation data sheets, sticky notes, and a pencil and writing board (a hard surface to lean on in the classroom). Not all log folder materials are used during each session. Only materials are used based on the issue of the day.

MAC PLC Evidence in Action

A MAC PLC is defined as having its focus on the cultivation of learning and interaction among teachers and administrators in order to improve teaching and learning outcomes for students (Hord, 2004; Kruse, Louis, & Bryk, 1995; McLaughlin & Talbert, 2006). The overarching goal of a PLC includes a constant creation of new knowledge within the organization and the aim of putting this new information into practice by using collaborative inquiry and reflection (Hord, 2004; Stoll & Louis, 2007). The following elements are considered:

- PLCs must concern themselves with certain structural elements such as who, what, where, when, why, and how teachers meet and participate in PLCs. An important aspect of the function of a PLC is to have appropriate allocated time for teachers to meet and collaborate.

- PLCs respect and encourage multiple perspectives and multiple competencies of all members participating in the PLC and the members that are being discussed.
- PLCs foster an increased sense of interconnectedness, belonging, community, and shared responsibility.
- It is through their long-term participation in the PLC that teachers generate new ideas and multiple perspectives from their interaction with their peers. Each school has a unique cultural context.

The following problem of practice is an example of a school that has taken steps to review successes and improve a challenge that reoccurs in the classroom. The process moves from identifying the problem of practice, creating a plan, implementing changes to solve the problem, and reflecting on the changes. This process is reflected in the following examples of a PLC, Instructional Round, and Lesson Study.

Example of the MAC PLC

Teachers and teacher leaders meet during a MAC PLC committee meeting at the School of Literacy. The School of Literacy was formed to help the student population that is an inner city school with the school population of mainly ELLs. Maranda, the teacher leader, is the leader to the PLC meeting. The teachers begin by receiving an agenda that states the problem that is going to be discussed. The agenda reads the following:

> *Problem of Practice:* The students that are 90% ELLs in the lower and upper school classes have difficulty writing across the content areas. The teachers implement writing workshop two days per week. However, the students are not making good progress and the state test scores show that students struggle with writing.

Michelle, Brenda, and Dave represent the lower and upper school classes. The teachers are using their planning time, an hourly session from 10:10 to 11:10 a.m., to conduct a MAC PLC. Since the problem of practice focuses on writing, the MAC PLC discussion targets this topic using the focus questions as a guide. The following events and conversations depict the MAC PLC meeting events:

Focus Question 1: Maranda, the teacher leader asks, "Teachers please give one example that you can remember when students integrated writing in math, reading, science, or social studies."

Michelle, the teacher of the Poets (grades K–1) answers the question: "My young children enjoy putting words on paper in any subject we study. I often ask them to write a sentence or two to describe something they enjoyed learning in the lesson. For example, Mary wrote in her Science Log after a seed planting lesson that she likes flowers and she can't wait to see the flowers pop out of the dirt. Mary also drew a pretty flower on the page."

Brenda, the teacher of the Scribes (grades 3–4), discussed the following: "My students like to write. They write in logs, journals and projects. In math class they write to solve problems. Each child writes the problem, writes the plan on how to solve the problem, writes the procedure that was followed and then writes how the solution was found. This is always a good writing assignment that gets students thinking."

Dave, the teacher of the Journalists (grades 5–6), shared the following information: "My Journalists love to write. They are always writing. However, they do not find writing to be easy. They struggle with putting sentences together that connect the main idea with details. I find that the students love to research on the Internet and then write about topics. When Rodney found information about the moon rover he decided to make a fact and fiction book about life on the moon. My student wrote, 'A moon rover is a space car and it was nicknamed Yugo during the first moon landing. . . . This car has special features such as flying, rolling over moon dust and climbing in craters.' This student loved writing about this topic," said Dave. "These topics really get my students writing."

Focus Question 2: Maranda then asked, "How do teachers and students support all students when writing?"

Dave mentioned, "I move around to each learner and conference with that student. I ask the student to read the draft to me and I ask questions about the draft." The other teachers agreed that they support students when writing by moving around the room and conferencing with each student.

Focus Question 3: Maranda asks, "How much time during the school day does each child write?"

Brenda explained, "I ask students to take out their author folders at least once or twice a week during the afternoon. There just isn't any other time for writing." The other teachers mentioned that writing is usually scheduled when they have the time. Writing usually takes place about once or twice per week.

Once the questions were discussed, Maranda pulled the group together and asked the teachers to reflect on how they might suggest ways to improve writing in classrooms. The teachers all agreed that writing should be done each day. If a child writes each day, he or she will be a better writer. Then, in a collective manner, Maranda asked the teachers to reflect on the rubric elements for PLC Team collaboration. Maranda asked the following: "Did we follow assigned roles?" Michelle stated, "I think we all followed our roles because we gave input to all questions." "Did we have everyone's participation?" Maranda asked. Dave yelled, "We all participated in a very professional and collaborative way by sharing our expertise. We even discussed the goal of the meeting by realizing that writing process needs to improve in our classrooms by having kids write more often!" Maranda stated, "Yes, I think we were very successful today."

Example of an Instructional Round Session

Bret, Derek, and Cathy each teach different multi-age groups in the School of Math, and each teacher has a different problem of practice that needs attention. During the pre-planning instructional round session, the research group decided to visit all three classrooms and observe, address issues, and then debrief about teaching.

There is some excitement in the air. Three teachers have volunteered to participate in an instructional round session. They prepare for the round's visit. Mr. Harry, the principal gives directions, "Okay team, some of us will be teaching a lesson and we will have the research group members observe us as we teach. How are we feeling today?" Derek says, "I can't wait to have this process begin. What I really want is to gain feedback on my teaching. That is a great thing."

Bret smiles and says, "I know we are going to be observed on just how we implement multi-age lesson components. I really can't wait for the feedback, but I am a bit nervous. The research group consists of teachers, the teacher leader, coach, principal, and even an outside consultant. Surely I will get information to help me move my teaching to the next effective level." Cathy adds to the conversation by saying, "I think our next step is to consider some focus questions so that the observers can collect information based on specific areas of need."

The teachers decide that they want the observers to collect data on the following focused questions:

Derek's question: How can I improve management of my multi-age classroom?
Cathy's question: What are the higher-order thinking processes that students are utilizing and what evidence do the team members observe?
Bret's question: How effective is the writing workshop for young students?

The teachers know that on the morning of the rounds, Mr. Harry, the principal, will meet with the members of the "walking team" for approximately twenty minutes to debrief about the protocols and what they will observe that day. The question each teacher created acts as the "problem of practice" and these questions are reviewed by the research team. Then, the team moves in each classroom to observe the teacher for 15 minutes. The team collects data based on the question. After the visits are completed in all classrooms, the research team conducts a debrief session to review the data collected. The team posts sticky notes on the charts on the wall. They place sticky notes under either the successes or challenges of each teacher under the teacher question. Then, the team analyzes the data. The team meets with each teacher at the end of the session to share the results of the instructional walk (Teitel, 2013).

The following data surfaced from each teacher observation of the Instructional Rounds:

Cathy

* Encourage teacher to use a variety of poems for all MAC students.
* Directions could be made clearer (some confusion).
* Tasks need to be connected coherently (avoid flipping around).

- Quality high-level thinking lesson questions are given during lesson when working with poetry and inferences.
- Students were engaged; good connection to prior knowledge.

Derek

- Classroom management is improving.
- Lesson objective was good.
- Needs to use manipulatives for lesson.
- Lack of higher-level questions.
- Too much teacher direction.
- Must use appropriate tasks for age group.
- Do not redraw examples; students had papers.
- Students were confused.

Bret

- Three ages in writing workshop. Used literature to teach lesson. Used author share time in a quality way to give feedback to each author.
- Referred to nouns in book. Could have used story nouns to connect to author stories.
- Too much noise—disorganization.
- Some students were done and sitting with nothing to do.
- Students should be conferenced with and given suggestions to continue writing.

The evidence that surfaced from each instructional round session helps each teacher to consider the strengths of the lesson and what changes should be made. This is an excellent way to embed professional development in the classroom and give input and feedback to the teacher in a nonthreatening way.

Example of Lesson Study

Lesson study is implemented in the MAC program following these steps:

- **Step 1:** Teachers come together to plan and share their ideas for how best to design the lesson by doing the following: drawing on their past experiences, making observations of their current students, and integrating their teacher's guide, their textbooks, and other resources. The end product is a lesson plan that describes in detail the design that the group has settled on for their lesson.
- **Step 2:** One teacher of the research group teaches the lesson to his or her students. This implementation is of a public nature because it involves the other teachers and administrators as observers. These observers come to the lesson with the lesson in hand, which they use as a tool to guide what they look for in the lesson. The research group moves around the class to view what each student is doing during the lesson. Each group member takes notes during the observation.
- **Step 3:** Debrief—after the lesson the research group comes together to reflect on the lesson they had seen unfold in a real classroom. Teachers and research-

ers share what they have observed as they watched the lesson and they provide reactions and suggestions.

- **Step 4:** Revising lesson—the revision process leads to the updated version of lesson after suggestions for improvement from the research group.
- **Step 5:** Teaching revised lesson—a second member of the group will publicly teach the lesson with revisions. Sometimes teachers will attend and observe the second and not the first lesson because it is a culmination of the group's work.
- **Step 6:** The group comes together to talk about two lessons and they list the strengths and weaknesses. A group member takes notes and then transforms the group's ideas into writing a report of their work.

SNAPSHOT OF A PRE-PLANNING STAGE FOR LESSON STUDY

Two teachers from the School of Literacy pre-planned a lesson based on the lesson study process with an outside consultant. The conversation follows:

Day 1

The Consultant: "I just wanted to reach out to see how you were doing. Did you and your colleagues get a chance to plan a lesson for the lesson study cycle on the first Friday of October? Did you agree on a common goal for the lesson study cycle? As we discussed, I am planning on visiting again October 22. Do you need any assistance before then?"

Day 2

The following data are the steps that were discussed to prepare for the lesson study to take place. The consultant and members of the lesson study group discuss the topic and steps that will be followed: "We are going to begin the lesson study cycle using Narrative Writing as our focus. Ellen, the teacher of the Poets (grades K–1) and Rosie the teacher of the Authors (grades 1–2) will work together to create a lesson. The following steps will be followed:

Consultant:

- Planning of the lesson will take place on Friday, November 6. (Just let me know the time so we can set up the phone conference.) Also we need to decide who will teach the first lesson as the research team observes.
- The actual teaching of the lesson will take place on Wednesday, November 11.
- Also on Wednesday, November 11, we will meet after and critique lesson observed and then plan the time for reteaching of the same lesson.
- I have attached the Multi-Age Lesson plan format to be used.

Our overall goal in this lesson study will be to introduce the students to Narrative Writing. The first lesson objectives are integrating the characteristics of personal narrative by discussing what makes a story interesting. Rosie will implement a lesson with the Authors (grades 1–2) which will include a mini lesson and then students will move around the room to write as authors. The teacher conferences with each student. Students' conference with other students. At the end of the lesson, authors volunteer to sit in the Author Chair and share their drafts. As each author shares, other authors give feedback, ask questions, and give the author suggestions for improving the story.

The lesson study team that included the principal, teacher, teacher leader, coach, and outside consultant observes the lesson. Following the lesson the team meets to debrief. Ellen will implement the second lesson in the unit the following day to the same class. She will incorporate suggestions made by team during the debriefing session. Following the second lesson, the lesson study team will meet to debrief again.

First Round of Lesson Study Process with Rosie (Teacher 1) (T1)

Lesson 1

Rosie, the teacher, presents a mini lesson on characterization. "Please write a story and think about what the character might say, do, and feel. Try to write about the character and describe these characteristics. Do you think using your senses will help you write about characters?" Mike, a student author responds with, "Yes, they help us to see things." "Okay, please go to any area in the room to write quietly. I will move around and see how each author is doing."

Debrief Session for Lesson One

Consultant (C) asked several questions to begin the debrief session that took place after implementation of the first lesson. The conversation was as follows:

C: Was the planning process effective?

T1: Yes, I liked planning with my colleague.

T2: It went well. But we don't spend enough time planning.

C: Did the long-term goals and lesson study goals help focus your lesson?

T1: I found that it helped scaffold the lesson activities.

T2: It also helped with planning the unit better.

C: Let's discuss our low inference notes from the lesson.

T2: I noticed all students' hands were raised when asked about the five senses but then

Consultant: How do the five senses connect to this lesson?

T1: I thought their senses would help them discover things about characters. That's why I told them don't worry all answers are good answers as long as we think.

T2: When T1 was working in the back with two students, five students were staring off into space. So I think it would be a good idea to give them some guidance of writing independently.

C: Let's discuss what revisions we can make for the second lesson.

C: Your mini lesson on characterization did not use any examples that students could follow. Do you think you could use a literature book to support the characterization qualities from a character in the book?

C: Why don't you target specific students to work with through the writing workshop? This will allow for differentiation of instruction.

C: Also try to promote student-centered activities. Students should be reading their pieces to each other.

T2: Like writing partners.

T1: So for differentiation we would need to analyze prior writing and pin point weaknesses in certain kid's right?

C: Also, after you read from literature, you did not discuss what makes this narrative writing interesting. You need to discuss with your students during the mini lesson the qualities that make effective narrative writing. Start with the storyline or plot. Point out how the story in the book has a beginning, middle, and end with a sequence of events. Then, ask them to give their examples about what the character does, says, and thinks.

Second Lesson Taught by Ellen, Teacher 2 (T2)

Ellen begins lesson. "Hi, authors. Today we have a special task. We need to write about a character that is interesting to read about. I would like you to think about what a character says and some actions the character displays. Let me read a few sentences from the book *Uncle Jed's Barbershop* by Margaree King Mitchell (1993). Please listen and tell me what you hear about one of the characters."

The teacher reads the following: "After Uncle Jed cut my daddy's hair, he lathered a short brush with soap and spread it over my daddy's face and shaved him."

Then, Ellen the teacher asked authors, "What are some things you learned about the character in the story? Okay, authors, please move to your writing space. If you need feedback you may ask a buddy to work with you. I will be conferencing with some of you in the classroom."

The following is a debrief session after the second lesson study was completed.

C: Let's start with the changes that were made to the second lesson and how students were affected by those changes.

T1: I noticed that because students listen to a story, they were able to think about how to describe the character.

T2: Yes, I used the literature book to help give an example.

T1: I also like how they were reading their work to one another. This made the lesson more student centered.

C: Yes. Students depended more on each other and the teacher was able to sit with a child and not be interrupted.

T2: And I reminded them that when they were having trouble students are allowed to ask their writing partners for help.

T1: Some of the stories were simple, but very interesting.

These conversations around the lesson study process are important. The lesson study process allows a team of teachers, principals, or consultants, to observe what students are doing and then discuss how to improve the lesson so that teachers consider just how to target personal needs of each learner.

The MAC program use strategies such as PLCs, Instructional Rounds, and Lesson Study to get teachers involved which also helps to encourage buy-in to the program. In this chapter we share evidence of the most effective strategies working with teachers, teacher leaders, and the school leadership. There is a clear, definable purpose for each of these strategies. The overarching purpose for all of these strategies is to look closely in classrooms to observe what teachers and students are doing.

The observations from teams generate a list of successes and challenges that are evident. Most importantly, this process focuses observations on student learning rather than on teachers teaching. It also helps to maintain nonjudgmental reflective conversations following these walk through observations. This information helps teachers to improve lesson implementation. This process also encourages careful planning of lessons (Kachur, Stout, & Edwards, 2013). The collaborative strategies that help teachers, teacher leaders, coaches, and administrators stay involved with school improvement have strategies (Kachur et al., 2013) that should be followed:

- Actively involve school teachers, teacher leaders, and school administrators to assist with informing, educating, and inspiring colleagues to become involved in the vision of the school program.
- Define and communicate the purpose of the walkthrough observations as a continuous school improvement process with a model that uses problems of practice to guide the professional development.

- Build trust with teachers and all staff by taking time to plan and introduce these strategies in a gradual way. This will help to spread the notion that these walk-through strategies have value when considering school improvement.
- Transparency is important when using these strategies in multi-age schools. Everyone should know the protocols to follow and what exactly to expect when participating in any one of these strategies. Trust and buy-in of these processes increase if teachers understand every part of the process.
- Provide training on how to collect data in a nonjudgmental way and then have debriefing conversations about the outcomes from the evidence that surface.
- A time for walkthrough observations should be built into the school schedule.
- The processes should be open to all teachers. This helps teachers and staff to understand the strategies.
- During these processes, encourage the team to focus on student learning. This gives information on how well students understand the concepts.
- These strategies are not used for punitive measures. The real objective is to encourage effective practices that should be shared by all teachers, teacher leaders' coaches, and administrators in the multi-age school.

EDUCATOR'S REFLECTION

Shared leadership strategies for reforming schools into multi-age programs are discussed in this chapter. Collaborative strategies such as PLCs, instructional rounds, and the lesson study processes bring school members together. This chapter presents a snapshot of such strategies in action by integrating program evidence. These strategies allow school educators to take ownership to the professional development process.

These reflective processes also build trust and allow teachers, teacher leaders, and principals to buy-in to the multi-age school agenda. Conversations help all members to grasp information about the program components, understand successes observed in classrooms, and target challenges that need to be improved. While instructional rounds, lesson study, and other observational tasks can take many different kinds of forms and numerous purposes, these collaborative walks through classrooms serve some purposes.

The purposes are to look to see if program components are implemented in a cohesive and successful way and review if instructional strategies support rigor in the classrooms. Rigor in the MAC program is defined as the following: teachers integrate multi-age components, students engage in active tasks and reasoning, teachers present concepts in multiple ways, teachers differentiate instruction to help personalize instruction, assessment is ongoing and students actively engage in questions and problems with other classmates regarding content understandings and concepts (Roberts, 2012). These collaborative strategies continue to encourage school staff to move from identifying the problem of practice, creating a plan, implementing changes to solve the problem, followed by reflecting on the changes.

APPLICATION OF CONCEPTS FOR ALL SCHOOL SYSTEMS

All school programs should encourage the following:

- Integrate the PLC process so that teachers create agendas to target "problems of practice" that surface.
- Instructional Rounds should be used at least three times per year to look closely in classrooms to observe how to improve problems in the school instructional program.
- Lesson Study should be integrated into a school program to allow teachers to collaborate on lesson implementation. This process allows teachers to share their expertise and cooperate on changing the weak areas of the teaching and learning process.
- Collaborative strategies allow staff to move from identifying the problem of practice, creating a plan, and implementing changes to solve the problem and followed by reflecting on the changes.

REFERENCES

Hord, S. M. (Ed.). (2004). *Learning together—leading together: Changing schools through learning communities.* New York, NY: Teachers College Press.

Kachur, D. S., Stout, J. A., & Edwards, C. L. (2013). *Engaging teachers in classroom walkthroughs.* Alexandria, VA: ASCD.

Kruse, S. D., Louis, K. S., & Bryk, A. (1995). An emerging framework for analyzing school-based professional community. In K. S. Louis & S. D. Kruse (Eds.), *Professionalism and community: Perspectives on reforming urban schools* (pp. 23–42). Thousand Oaks, CA: Corwin Press.

McLaughlin, M. W., & Talbert, J. E. (2006). *Building school-based teacher learning communities: Professional strategies to improve student achievement.* New York, NY: Teachers College Press.

Mitchell, M. K. (1993). *Uncle Jed's barbershop.* New York, NY: Scholastic.

Roberts, J. E. (2012). *Instructional rounds in action.* Cambridge, MA: Harvard Education Review.

Stoll, L., & Louis, K. S. (Eds.). (2007). *Professional learning communities: Divergence, depth, and dilemmas.* Glasgow: McGraw-Hill.

Teitel, L. (2013). *School-based instructional rounds: Improving teaching and learning across classroom.* Cambridge, MA: Harvard Education Press.

10

Multi-Age Learning Community Professional Development Plan

Methods of Assessing Organization Support and Change

Cally is a multi-age teacher. She really enjoys her job. She loves to share ideas with other teachers, plan lessons together, and participate in opportunities to improve her performance with her students. Cally has a discussion with other teachers about their successes that they have in the program implementation. Cally says, "How are we doing? How do we know we are doing what we need to do to help our students succeed?" Jared responds by saying, "I am not sure if our PLC meetings work. The meetings have the right agendas. And, we do discuss the issues." Cally responds to Jared by saying, "I think we are moving ahead, but we need some evidence that tells us we are doing good things that are successful in the program. Let us discuss this issue with Ms. Erik (principal) and others."

These teachers have a right to know how the program implementation is working. They also should see evidence that helps them understand the successes of the program and the challenges. The teachers need feedback on how to improve practices.

MULTI-AGE LEARNING COMMUNITY PROFESSIONAL DEVELOPMENT PLAN

The goal of the multi-age school program is to help schools and districts develop effective and powerful teaching and learning on a broad scale, in order to target the needs of all learners. For this to happen, the learning from this multi-age school transformation must become more than just an effective professional development program for educators. Improvement on a large scale for school systems requires going beyond teachers and administrators working as a shared leadership team in a school to address the needs of individual learners. Some schools do that already.

What multi-age schools need to do is to rethink the traditions of schooling. Do school classrooms target the needs of each learner by using basal readers and textbook pacing guides for grade level requirements? Do classrooms need to address curriculum learning targets by teaching all students in the class the same information, at the same pace, and in the same way? Do teachers have the authority to give information to students, rather than allow each student to collaborate and cooperate with peers, sharing knowledge and grasping ideas through interactive problem-solving events? The short answer to these questions is—by itself—no.

The important question to ask is: Do we allow all students to perform as independent learners and thinkers so that they may build on their cognitions in personal and meaningful ways? This chapter presents the methods of assessing organizational support and change through evidence.

The multi-age programs will not singlehandedly lead to better teaching, learning, and high achieving outcomes. Educators should understand that a multi-age program is an exceptional and powerful accelerant of school program improvement that helps to target individual needs of the learner. The program builds the curriculum around what the student needs and not force curriculum on the student.

PROFESSIONAL DEVELOPMENT PLAN

This chapter outlines a multi-age school professional development plan that assists school districts and schools map out how multi-age programs might connect to their school community. Professional development is a very important aspect for improving school systems. If professional development is not available for teachers and administrators the outcome of the new program often fails. This plan explains how this process is introduced to district, school, and parent communities. Also, this chapter integrates a discussion about program evidence that is collected ongoing during multi-age school events.

MAKING DISTRICT CHANGES TO BRING ON INSTRUCTIONAL IMPROVEMENT

Districts trying to make instructional changes and going beyond isolated pockets of need should consider four important elements of excellence (City, Elmore, Fiarman, & Teitel, 2010) that can apply to the multi-age philosophy:

- Design a multi-age perspective that clearly supports what high-quality teaching and learning looks like in your district—a view that all members of the district agree on that will help to improve the instructional core.
- Construct a collaborative and cooperative learning school district that integrates a multi-age culture that gains support from all members of the district. To be

successful in facilitating quality student learning that encourages high-level thinking, problem solving, and collaboration, districts must and should encourage adults to develop these same skills.

- Generate and implement coherent district-wide strategies that support multi-age teaching and learning agendas that the district wants in school buildings and classrooms. This means to present a broad picture of how the program will connect to the district schools and then begin an implementation plan that integrates program strategies slowly. A vision action plan can be a good way to start.

- Organize a system that aligns the allocation of human and financial resources and district support to the multi-age program strategies.

A district should put in place an accountability system in order to achieve success in the implementation of the multi-age program. The following is an example of how a school district moved ahead with the introduction of the multi-age school program agenda. The superintendent scheduled a meeting with all district leaders and school principals.

During the meeting an outside consultant presented the multi-age program philosophy, program components, and real-to-life episodes of how school systems integrate the multi-age teaching and learning community into the district schools. Any questions that district administrators had were answered during the event. Questions, conversations, and concerns that surfaced during the meeting follows:

- *Principal 1:* "I think the multi-age philosophy targets just what we need in schools today, however, how do I get my school community to understand this is a good way to offer education to our students?"

  Consultant: "All school community members such as administrators, teachers, parents and students should be introduced to the program components. All school district members must be involved early on in the process."

- *Assistant Superintendent of Curriculum and Instruction:* "What type of resource allocations should we consider for this multi-age program?"

  Consultant: "We need to have human and financial support from the district. What this means is that we need appropriate qualified teachers that are willing to make changes and we need financial support such as time for planning the program implementation and having adequate instructional materials in all school buildings."

- *Principal 2:* "How can I inform my staff of just how this multi-age program will impact my school environment?"

  Consultant: "I suggest that workshops be given on an ongoing basis to give appropriate support to teachers, administrators and staff. Also, I suggest that schools begin by having conversations with their staff on just how this multi-age program can fit into the school program. It is best if the program starts slowly in a few grades. However, some schools do elect to change the whole school environment at once so that everyone is doing the same things. I have seen both approaches succeed."

Developing a Clear and Articulate Agenda for High-Quality Teaching and Learning

Teachers tend to have very different points of view on instruction. It is important to present an explicit and widely held view of what constitutes quality teaching and learning in the school setting and then present just how a multi-age program connects to those views. The first step is to have conversations with school teachers in each school of the district to reflect on what their approach to good teaching and learning means in their school building. During an initial school building teacher meeting with a consultant, the following conversations took place:

- *Teacher 1:* "I do not understand why we need multi-age students. We are doing just fine in our classrooms with the graded system. We teach based on our textbook curriculum and pacing guides and we cover all the topics in the books by the end of the year."

  Consultant: "Unfortunately, our schools are not doing well to educate our students for the 21st century. We need to encourage problem solvers, collaborators, high level thinkers, leaders, and technological advanced students so that they leave school with the skills for the workplace. Do you think your textbook curriculum addresses these 21st-century skills?"
- *Teacher 2:* "How will our parents feel about this multi-age program?"

  Consultant: "Training should be offered to parents on a regular basis. Parents should be asked to participate in this program as active school members. What this means is that parents will have a role in supporting a caring and trusting school environment by visiting classrooms and sharing their own expertise, helping with class events, supporting their students during outside tasks, and making sure that their children are taking on homework responsibilities."

Ongoing Professional Development for a Multi-Age School Program

There are specific professional development components that are offered to implement a successful multi-age program. Professional development is an ongoing process. To initiate such a program, it usually takes about three years.

The first year, members of the school are introduced to all program components. In the first year, some schools begin to change to multi-age learning in place of traditional components. The second year, most of the multi-age program components are embedded into the daily school schedule. And, the third year, all components are in place and teachers only ask for support, when necessary.

The professional development model includes the following: an annual three-day summer academy, monthly principal workshops, monthly teacher support workshops, an outreach coaching program in classrooms, and monthly parent workshops.

MAC PROGRAM COMPONENTS AND METHODS OF ASSESSING ORGANIZATIONAL SUPPORT

The methods of assessing the organization support system are the following:

- Direct observations in the school environment
- Reflective journals
- PLC rubric
- Focus group sessions
- Analysis of school records
- Field notes/coaching logs
- Principal walkthroughs
- Site-based committee meetings
- Parent survey

Three-Day Summer Academy

The three-day summer academy is an all-day workshop model where components of the multi-age program are presented in a hands-on manner during a conversation style atmosphere (see table 10.1). In Year 1, the summer academy agenda introduces the participants to all program components.

Table 10.1. Agenda for Summer Academy Year 1

Monday, August 19	Tuesday, August 20	Wednesday, August 21
8:15–8:30 am Breakfast	**8:15–8:30 am** Breakfast	**8:15–8:30 am** Breakfast
8:30–8:45 am Introductions	**8:30–10:00 am** Thirteen Years of a Multi-Age Program, *Guest Speaker, Principal*	**8:30–9:30 am** Investigations (Learning Centers)
8:45–9:00 am Survey/ Needs Assessment		
9:00–10:00 am Introduction of Multi-age Program Components	**10:00–11:15 am** Reading Process—Multi-Age Programs	**9:30–11:00 am** Common Core State Standards in Multi-Age Programs
10:00–10:15 am Break	**11:15 am–12:15 pm** Interdisciplinary Theme Plan/Teaching	**11:00 am–12:30 pm** Setting up the Digital Backpack for Multi-Age Classrooms
10:15–11:00 am Assessment in Multi-Age Classes	**12:15–12:30 pm** Lunch	**12:30–12:45 pm** Lunch
11:00 am–12:00 pm Finding Your Vision— Collaboration, PLC	**12:30–1:15 pm** Focus Group Session	**12:45–1:15 pm** Focus Group Session
12:00–12:30 pm Lunch		
12:30–1:15 pm Focus Group Session		

Year 2, the components are presented in very specific ways and the implementations of the components are carefully investigated by teachers and administrators. In Year 3, all components of the program are reviewed and discussions are focused on areas that are difficult for teachers to implement.

Outreach Program in Schools

Consultants and coaches visit the school once or twice per month. Each session begins with a mini lesson on a program component or strategy. Then, observations are completed in all classrooms. The coach observes classrooms and completes a Field Note Worksheet as in figure 10.1. Field notes are anecdotal comments that are used to assess how well multi-age program components are implemented during lessons.

In figure 10.1, the coach presents a good description of how the classroom setting is organized and which instructional practices are applied successfully. The coach writes down the areas that need improvement.

After the class observation is completed by the coach, the teacher is contacted for a brief meeting. During the debrief meeting, the teacher learns of the successes and areas of improvement taken from the observation. During the month, the principal conducts walkthroughs on an informal level. Once again, the principal is observing

FIELD NOTES   Coach Observer: Ms. Star   Teacher: 4-5 mathematics

Thursday: 10/16/14   Field Notes

The classroom was arranged with 3 groups of students' desks organized for collaborative work and one small group of students were at the desk facing the board; they were waiting for the teacher to teach them a lesson on percent. A second group was working on fractions, and the third group was completing algorithms with multiplication of whole numbers. The teacher said that she tried to meet with each group each day and also circulate to help students with their work.

General Notes: The teacher asked that I come to her math class to give feedback on her teaching. The set-up of the classroom was good, as groupings of students were easily rearranged. Students knew that when they were finished with direct instruction, they returned to their group and worked on the concept that was taught in the mini lesson. The teacher can now use some help in making sure that the three groups are working on the same concept on different levels. The teacher mentioned she enjoyed teaching in a multi-age classroom. I, as coach, observed that students were on task and working on solving math problems.

Figure 10.1.   Field Note Worksheet

just how the program components are implemented successfully. The MAC Walk-through Checklist is used by the principal during short visits to classrooms during the month (see appendix A). This walkthrough often supports the coach's observation field notes. For example, the principal writes down on a walkthrough checklist that the teacher he is observing should think about the following: *The teacher should consider how to offer learners a differentiated approach using a variety of effective tasks. These tasks should reteach the same concept on different levels.*

Lesson Plan

All lesson plans should follow the multi-age lesson format (see appendix D). Components of the lesson include the following: Essential questions that guide the lesson. These questions are always posted in the classroom so that students understand the expectations of the lesson objectives, procedures, higher-level thinking strategies, differentiated tasks, and formative assessments. The Common Core State Standards are listed based on three grade levels to accommodate levels for all learners. Teachers are asked to have the lesson plans available for coaches during observations and for principals during walkthroughs. This lesson plan document supports the strategies that are being implemented at the time of the observation.

OTHER ASSESSMENT TOOLS FOR COLLECTING DATA WITH SUPPORTING EVIDENCE (FOR THREE YEARS)

Focus Group

Participants take part in a Focus Group session during the Summer Academy. The purpose of the Focus Group is to understand the perspectives of the teachers, teacher leaders, and administrators based on the program components presented at the workshop. The Focus Group meets three times (once per day), for approximately 45 minutes each. At the meeting, the participants in the study share information and they give feedback based on the researcher's prompts. The session is audio recorded and transcribed and focus group notes are taken. The following evidence summarizes just how participants felt during the three year program based on the four focus group questions:

Question 1: Do you feel comfortable with the multi-age planning process based on what you have learned in the program?

Year 1

> *Teacher 1:* I'm still a little iffy about this multi-age agenda. I'm doing multi-age now with grades 2–3 ELA and also with 4–5. They are two different groups of four different grades. So, I'm excited but also nervous.

Teacher 2: There is an enormous amount of planning time. Our principal indicated that she was trying to arrange for two hours of planning twice per week. She suggested that we use PLC time to also plan with our team. PLC meets once per week. I really need more time for planning!!!

Year 2

Teacher 1: You learn as you do it. You make mistakes as you go. It is a fun process and teachers become friends.
Teacher 2: Having outside consultants is a great asset. The planning process is fine. We are comfortable. We are going along with learning by sharing.

Year 3

Teacher 1: We started working on learning targets last year. Now going forward, I have a better understanding of how to start with that.
Teacher 2: I now feel going through the workshops gives us the experience. This program is not too dramatically different in the approach.

Reading these focus group responses of teachers allows us to see a trend that surfaces; how teachers felt discomfort in the first year, the second year feeling more comfortable with planning and the third year the teachers feel more confident. One teacher stated that the multi-age program is not dramatically different from what she is used to.

Question 2: What strengths do you believe your school has that will influence the program based on what you have learned?

Year 1

Teacher 1: I have to say that our principal is very much into this and her enthusiasm is contagious: She is all for PLCs. We have excellent leadership support.
Teacher 2: Staff is creative and excited to learn.

Year 2

Teacher 1: You make mistakes as you go. Tons of ideas to use.
Teacher 2: Collaboration of teachers.

Year 3

Teacher 1: We are working more collectively and collaboratively.
Teacher 2: Parents liked the idea of the other students being mentors.

Question 3: What resources do you think you will need?

Year 1

> *Teacher 1:* We need more parent support.
> *Teacher 2:* Lots of manipulatives. Theme ideas and theme days will strengthen the school. The program will introduce little kids to bigger kids.

Year 2

> *Teacher 1:* Smart Board for multi-age.
> *Teacher 2:* Authors' study.

Year 3

> *Teacher 1:* Information for parents is needed.
> *Teacher 2:* Getting more information on the readers and writers workshop.

Question 4: What are some challenges?

Year 1

> *Teacher 1:* Need more technology.
> *Teacher 2:* Need time and flexibility.

Year 2

> *Teacher 1:* Information for parents.
> *Teacher 2:* Time to meet PLCs.

Year 3

> *Teacher 1:* We need to visit other schools.
> *Teacher 2:* Going into year 3, we have faculty that will try anything.

These focus group sessions were meaningful. The comments give a clear indication of just how teachers and other members of the program felt going through the three-year process. It seems that each year served as a stepping stone to the next year. The summer academy was more useful as the years moved ahead. The professional development program made teachers and staff rethink things by considering how the teachers would change in their practices when offering a more effective program for students.

Journals

Teachers in MAC are asked to keep an ongoing journal. These reflective writings help to keep track of the attitudes and perspectives of teachers based on the program training and the implementation process. The following sample journals are examples of teachers' voices over a period of three years. When analyzing the journals, it is evident that the trend over three years shows that teachers feel uneasy when implementing program components in Year 1, more sure of the program tasks in Year 2, and they express excitement of the implementation of the program by Year 3.

Year 1

> *October:* After returning to 20 minutes or so of traditional teaching, I've noticed students began adjusting to the new style of (multi-age) learning when targeting each student's needs. We are progressing, having fun, creating projects and I've already covered more this year than I did last year. Student learning and improvement is evident. I'm still faced with the challenges of how to meet the needs of each student. Multi-age classrooms take time planning.
>
> *December:* Over the last two weeks, I am finally beginning to see progress and improvement from all of my students. Students are asking friends for help and the children are becoming leaders on all levels.
>
> *March:* I am really happy that all students like their novels and are eager to read. That is always a good sign for teachers to observe. I am implementing more about academic vocabulary and informational text which seems to work well in my lessons. This week I am going to have the students rotate through stations to target different levels of understanding in my class. I think they are at the point that they can handle, especially the advance students. They will be focusing on story board, plot, character point of view, and cause and effect. I really like how the stations give me time to spend with those students who need my help. The guided reading is really helping the students show their comprehension.

Year 2

> *October:* Multi-age went very well in my class last week. We started a new unit on money. This unit is perfect for both age groups of primary students since it meets both standards well. The money unit also allows ways for students to learn a tough topic, but play games while they are learning this topic. I look forward to this week during math class to doing more multi-age centers based on money objectives.

March: I have worked out a system that has been working very nicely in keeping my students organized and responsible during activity centers. Each week, they have the goal of completing three of six activity centers. I assign them the first center in order to be sure that each student is working on the skills that he/she most needs. Students then are provided the opportunity to choose between two teacher directed options for their next center. The process continues over a three-day period. One of the options students can complete after they have completed the mandatory three centers is "Your Choice." Here students may choose any of the Activity Centers in the classroom. To provide the students with further responsibility and independence, each student is supplied with a file folder and a Completion Sheet. When the activity is completed, the box is colored in on the sheet and the recording sheet is placed in the student's personal file. This allows students to return to unfinished activity centers, to track their own progress, and provides practice with time management.

Year 3

June: All groups have a variety of learning levels. I have implemented a strong routine and learning structure for them. They were not use to that, but now they have picked up on the program's expectations, as well as mine. Reading focuses on guided group/individual/informational text/leveled readers and novels. Station work reflects the CCS skills that are to be reached. All lessons are interactive and level based.

Analyses of the Minutes from Site-based Program Meetings

The agendas and minutes from site visit committee meetings and follow up sessions include detailed descriptions of the issues and the nature of the interactions during the professional development outreach program (Guskey, 2000). Each meeting targets specific components to the MAC program. For example, Lesson Study, Interdisciplinary Unit Planning, and a discussion about the role of teacher leader in the school, are just one day's agenda of the Site Visit Report (see figure 10.2).

Parent Survey

The role of parents is an important aspect of the program. Parents must be informed about what the MAC program is about, why it is useful for learners, and how the program will affect their role as parents in the school. MAC offers a parent workshop once per month.

Date: Thursday, December 5, 2013
Time: 8:30 a.m.–2:00 p.m.
Meeting Objectives:
   1.   Determine a central idea for an interdisciplinary unit, using the ecosystem resources.
   2.   Plan a timeline to develop the interdisciplinary unit and to present it to the wider community.
Meeting Agenda:
   1.   Meet and discuss agenda for the meetings
   2.   Meet with all teachers to discuss the progress on the interdisciplinary theme
   3.   Discuss progress on personal reflection journals
   4.   Establish a timeline for implementation of the unit
   5.   Identify other issues to be clarified
Meeting Outcomes (next steps):
   1.   Teachers and students gave a concrete demonstration of how interdisciplinary teaching and
        learning is working within their school. The team watched a presentation by students on several
        different and interdisciplinary aspects of oil and natural gas. Students worked as a coherent team
        with appropriate division of responsibilities. Students demonstrated very good presentation skills
        and higher order thinking. Students conducted research on the topic and they demonstrated very
        good knowledge of the subject matter. Teachers did a very good job of facilitating the
        presentation.
   2.   The team met with all teachers to discuss progress on interdisciplinary theme. The teachers
        discussed the progress they have made on the theme of ecosystems and community. They
        discussed the roles and titles for their classrooms: Discoverers, Investigators, Explorers, and
        others.
   3.   PK-4Teachers said their collaboration was coming along fine. They said they need to continue to
        collaborate more to better plan appropriate learning activities. They need planning time to
        collaborate. 5-8 teachers said that the lessons are taught in isolation, but the teachers are all
        following the same theme. Planning time is needed with 5-8 teachers.
   4.   Teachers said they need to have students investigate and focus on higher-order questions related
        to the ecosystems and their community. This will allow students to learn how to do research own
        their own. Teachers will help students to identify resources for students to use: public library,
        Internet, persons with particular expertise like the mayor, and local newspapers. The principal
        was encouraged to give some planning time during the week to teachers so that collaboration is
        encouraged for planning theme lessons.
   5.   Schedule follow-up meetings
   6.   For next meeting:
        a.   Collect their vision action plans and their curriculum maps and schedules for block
             scheduling and PLC meetings
        b.   Get teaching reflection journals from teachers
        c.   Review curriculum maps

Figure 10.2.   Site Visit Report

Parents' roles are to connect to the classroom events as much as possible. This means that parents should visit classrooms to read books, volunteer during lessons, get involved with fund raising projects, and support their child at home with projects and daily homework tasks. Parents are given a Parent Survey on occasion in order to document just how parents feel about the program implementation. The following sample survey questions and results from one multi-age school are as follows (see table 10.2).

From the results of this survey, parents think that learners working in cooperative tasks are meaningful. Also, parents feel that they want to be kept informed of

Table 10.2.   Parent Survey Responses and Results

Item	% Agree/ Strongly Agree
I have high expectations for my child in a multi-age class. (4.36)	82%
Give my child meaningful assignments that help him or her learn. (4.64)	91%
Keeps me informed about my child's academic progress. (4.36)	91%
Keeps me informed about what my child is learning. (4.18)	91%
How do you feel about different age groups working together?	73%
How do you feel about children learning with themes? (4.36)	91%
How do you feel about children working in skill groups (students are grouped and regrouped according to specific goals, activities, and individual needs)? (4.36)	91%
How do you feel about children learning in cooperative groups? (4.63)	100%
Is MAC preparing my child well to be promoted to the next level? (4.54)	82%

what the student is learning, the child's progress, and which themes are studied. The parents are somewhat concerned about the learner working with different age groups. Parents are concerned if the learner is well prepared to be promoted to the next grade.

These weaknesses can be overcome if the teachers keep parents informed on the benefits for students when they work with different age groups. Some learners become leaders, others students receive extra help from peers, and they all learn from each other.

Multi-Age Professional Learning Community Continuum Rubric

The Multi-Age PLC Continuum Rubric assesses the actual implementation of the PLC process. It provides a breakdown of crucial elements (overall PLC development, mission, shared vision, shared values, goals, collaborative culture, parent partnerships, action research, continuous improvement, and a focus on results). The rubric also provides information needed to best meet the needs of the participants in the academy. The assessment is given in the beginning of the academy, at the end of the first year, second year, and third year.

PLC rubric data from one specific multi-age school for a three-year period is as follows (see table 10.3): teachers showed an overall high level of collective responsibility to improve the school on all levels (4.68) in questions 1–7 and lower levels of reflective dialogue (3.16) in questions 8–11 and very low deprivatized practices (1.55) in questions 12–15. The staff is in close alignment with shared sense of purpose (4.14), peer collaboration (4.12), and a strong focus on student learning (4.43).

What this evidence means is that teachers in this school worked well together and felt that they needed to collaborate on all school issues. However, teachers did not feel comfortable reflecting on issues some of the time. This weak area shows

Table 10.3. Multi-Age Teacher Professional Community Survey

Please answer the following questions using the scales provided. Circle your answer.					
1. How many teachers in this school help maintain discipline in the entire school, not just the classroom?	none	some	about half	most	nearly all
2. How many teachers in this school take responsibility for improving the school?	none	some	about half	most	nearly all
3. How many teachers in this school set high standards for themselves?	none	some	about half	most	nearly all
4. How many teachers in this school are eager to try new ideas?	none	some	about half	most	nearly all
5. How many teachers in this school feel responsible for helping students develop self-control?	none	some	about half	most	nearly all
6. How many teachers in this school feel responsible to help each other do his/her best?	none	some	about half	most	nearly all
7. How many teachers in this school feel responsible that all students learn?	none	some	about half	most	nearly all
8. How often do you typically have conversations with your colleagues about what helps students learn best?	less than once a month	two or three times a month	once or twice a week	almost daily	daily
9. How often do you typically have conversations with colleagues about development of new curriculum?	less than once a month	two or three times a month	once or twice a week	almost daily	daily

10. How often do you typically have conversations with colleagues about the goals of this school?	less than once a month	two or three times a month	once or twice a week	almost daily	daily
11. How often do you typically exchange suggestions for curriculum materials with colleagues?	less than once a month	two or three times a month	once or twice a week	almost daily	daily
12. How often do you typically visit other teachers' classrooms to observe instruction?	less than once a month	two or three times a month	once or twice a week	almost daily	daily
13. How often do you typically receive meaningful feedback on your performance from colleagues?	less than once a month	two or three times a month	once or twice a week	almost daily	daily
14. How often do you typically have other colleagues observe your classroom?	less than once a month	two or three times a month	once or twice a week	almost daily	daily
15. How often do you typically invite someone to help teach your classes?	less than once a month	two or three times a month	once or twice a week	almost daily	daily
16. Most of my colleagues share my beliefs and values about what the central mission of the multi-age school should be.	strongly disagree	disagree	neither agree nor disagree	agree	strongly agree

(continued)

Table 10.3. *(Continued)*

Please answer the following questions using the scales provided. Circle your answer.					
17. Goals and priorities for the multi-age school are clear.	strongly disagree	disagree	neither agree nor disagree	agree	strongly agree
18. In this school the teacher and administration are in close agreement on school discipline policy.	strongly disagree	disagree	neither agree nor disagree	agree	strongly agree
19. The principal, teachers, and staff collaborate to make this school run effectively.	strongly disagree	disagree	neither agree nor disagree	agree	strongly agree
20. Teachers design instructional programs together.	strongly disagree	disagree	neither agree nor disagree	agree	strongly agree
21. Teachers at this school make a conscious effort to coordinate their teaching with instruction at other grade levels.	strongly disagree	disagree	neither agree nor disagree	agree	strongly agree
22. Most teachers in this school are cordial.	strongly disagree	disagree	neither agree nor disagree	agree	strongly agree
23. The school really works at developing students' social skills.	strongly disagree	disagree	neither agree nor disagree	agree	strongly agree
24. When making important decisions, the school always focuses on what's best for student learning.	strongly disagree	disagree	neither agree nor disagree	agree	strongly agree
25. The school has well defined learning expectations for all students.	strongly disagree	disagree	neither agree nor disagree	agree	strongly agree
26. The school sets high standards for academic performance.	strongly disagree	disagree	neither agree nor disagree	agree	strongly agree
27. The school day is organized to maximize	strongly disagree	disagree	neither agree nor disagree	agree	strongly agree

that teachers did not visit classrooms to gain new ideas or input on practices. This weakness can be improved when a school encourages teachers to become active participants in the instructional rounds and lesson study processes. These processes embed classroom visitation, observations, and dialogue to gain insight into what teachers are doing well and not well.

EDUCATOR'S REFLECTION

The professional development components presented in this chapter are significant for making the change to a multi-age program. There are real-to-life situations that are shared in this chapter that are helpful ideas for school districts and school buildings. Also, an important aspect to this program is to collect evidence ongoing. This evidence should be analyzed and shared with the school community. The samples of evidence for the program included in this chapter are some ways to collect data. It is important to use data to understand the successes and the challenges that surface and then make improvements.

APPLICATION OF CONCEPTS FOR ALL SCHOOL SYSTEMS

All school programs should encourage the following:

- Integrate the appropriate professional development components to the school district and school building that target the professional development agendas.
- Use appropriate evidence to analyze program components. This will help with improving the processes of the program.

REFERENCES

City, E. A., Elmore, R. F., Fiarman, S. E., & Teitel, L. (2010). *Instructional rounds in education: A network approach to improving teaching and learning.* Cambridge, MA: Harvard Education Press.
Guskey, T. R. (2000). *Evaluating professional development.* Thousand Oaks, CA: Corwin Press.

APPENDIXES

Rowman & Littlefield has made the appendixes included in this book available as a single PDF formatted for easy and clear printing on 8.5" × 11" paper. Download a PDF of all the appendixes for *The Multi-Age Learning Community in Action* by accessing the "Features" tab on the Rowman & Littlefield book page: https://rowman.com/ISBN/9781475837759.

Appendix A

Principal Walkthrough Checklist

MAC Elements	Strategies	Strategies Noticed?		Observation Questions and Comments
		YES ☑	No ☑	
PLANNING	Classroom Management targeting learning expectations for the lesson, day, week			
LITERACY ACROSS THE CURRIC. 1. Reading Strategies 2. Math and Problem Solving 3. Writing Workshop	Reading Strategies a. Activate prior knowledge b. Predicting c. Think-alouds d. Reflect and summarize e. Chants and poems f. Use artifacts/inquiry discovery learning			
MATH	Math and Problem Solving a. Whole group (< 20 mins) b. Small group (problem-solving process) c. Scaffolding work: flexible grouping targeting individual needs d. Independent work			

LITERACY	a. Interactive Shared Reading
	b. Close reading
	c. Scaffold reading
	d. Literature circles
	  i. Collaborative learning
	  ii. Peer-assisted learning
	e. Independent reading
	f. Writing workshop (using evidence from information text)			

WRITING	Writing Workshop a. Use a variety of authentic literature, poetry, and nonfiction books b. Give mini lesson based on purpose c. Allow students to write every day d. Use the writing process				

INQUIRY-BASED LEARNING
1. Inquiry teaching and learning
	a. Discovery lessons
	b. Hypothesis testing
	  i. Guide
	  ii. Explore
	  iii. Investigate
	  iv. Conclude/debrief				

ASSESSMENT	a. Diagnostic: Pretests, on-demand writing b. Formative: Journal entries, peer-reviews, self-reflection assignments, portfolios c. Summative: midterm, final project, paper				
Interdisciplinary Studies	Connection to subject areas				
Learning Centers	Connection to subject areas				
Differentiated Teaching and Learning	Connection to subject areas				

Source: Adapted from Downey, C. J., Steffy, B. E., English, F. W., Frase, L. E., & Poston, W. K., Jr. (2004). *The three-minute classroom walk-through: Changing school supervisory practice one teacher at a time.* Thousand Oaks, CA: Corwin Press.

Appendix B

Action Plan

Multi-age Learning Community School Mission Statement:

Multi-age Learning Community School Vision:

Multi-age Learning Community School Theme:

Multi-age Learning Community Goal:				
MAC Objective	Action to Be Taken	Participants	Time Frame	Assessment

Appendix C

Curriculum Map

	OCTOBER	NOVEMBER	DECEMBER
Essential Topics to Cover			
Core Standards			

(continued)

Appendix C

	OCTOBER	NOVEMBER	DECEMBER
Content			
Concepts			
Process Skills			
Assessments			

	OCTOBER	NOVEMBER	DECEMBER
Activities			
Describe Active Learning Strategies, Child Centered, Project-based Tasks			
Vocabulary			
Resources Used			

(continued)

	OCTOBER	NOVEMBER	DECEMBER
Higher-Level Thinking			
Technology Used			
Miscellaneous/Notes			

Source: Adapted from Truesdale, V., Thompson, C., & Lucas, M. (2004). Use of curriculum mapping to build a learning community. In H. H. Jacobs (Ed.), *Getting results with curriculum mapping*. Alexandria, VA: ASCD.

Appendix D

Lesson Plan Format

LESSON TOPICS

Unit Essential Questions

1.

2.

3.

Common Core State Standards
Use Multigrade Standards

Lesson Objectives	Assessments
1.	1.
2.	2.

Step-by-Step Lesson Procedures and Tasks
1.
2.
3.
4.
Differentiated Instructional Practices
Higher-Level Thinking
Resources Needed

Source: Adapted from Tomlinson C. A., & McTighe, J. (2006). *Integrating differentiated instruction and understanding by design: Connecting content and kids.* Alexandria, VA: ASCD.

Appendix E

Coaching Log

School:_____ Principal:_____ Teacher:_____ Coach: _____

Goal 1: _____

Goal 2: _____

Coaching Sessions

Date	Goal Addressed	Discussion Notes	Next Steps	Evidence of Progress	Concerns

Appendix F

Class Field Notes Form

SCHOOL: _____   CLASS:_____
OBSERVER: _____   TEACHER: _____
DATE: _____   TIME: _____

****

FIELD NOTES	PERSONAL PERCEPTIONS

Appendix G

Classroom Observation Checklist

Teacher(s)_____Multi-age Grade Configuration _____

Observer:_____ School:_____ Date:_____

Rate the teacher on a scale of 0 – 5 (0 lowest score/5 highest score) – consider what student is doing

Describe the setting that is observed: _____

During the multi-age class observation, the following elements are present – consider teacher, class environment, and what students are doing:	0	1	2	3	4	5
Demonstrate knowledge of best practices of content, concepts, skills using Common Core Standards integration Notes:						
Apply quality strategies such as collaborative behavior, flexible grouping, differentiated learning Notes:						
Integrates process learning practices: process writing, literature-based reading, problem solving math, hands-on tasks in subjects, project-based activities, inquiry learning Notes:						

Teacher(s)_____Multi-age Grade Configuration _____

Observer:_____ School:_____ Date:_____

Rate the teacher on a scale of 0 – 5 (0 lowest score/5 highest score) – consider what student is doing

During the multi-age class observation, the following elements are present – consider teacher, class environment, and what students are doing:	0	1	2	3	4	5
Aligns formative assessment strategies in lesson Notes:						
Implement interdisciplinary theme lesson Notes:						
Implement Investigations (learning centers) Notes:						
Other (problem-solving) Notes:						

Appendix H

Teaching Journal

Name: _____   *Date:* _____

1. What strategies have you integrated into your classroom from the Summer Academy?

2. Describe the success you have in the classroom.

3. Show evidence of the success.

4. What are some challenges you have in the classroom?

5. How can the MAC (Multi-Age Classroom) team assist you?

Index

About the Author

Barbara Cozza, PhD, is an associate professor, assistant chairperson, and program director for the EdD in Instructional Leadership, in the Department of Administrative and Instructional Leadership at St. John's University, Queens, New York.

Dr. Cozza's research targets school reform issues in the areas of curriculum, instruction, assessment, and leadership. Current research investigates how to improve and transform school systems into vital programs looking closely at shared leadership agendas and at the instructional core for regular education students and ELLs. The investigations integrate strategies such as PLCs, leadership coaching, teacher leadership, instructional rounds, lesson study, and multi-age teaching and learning programs. Dr. Cozza works with teachers and administrators throughout the United States and internationally to develop more collaborative partnerships to improve educational systems, in and out of the classroom.

Currently, Dr. Cozza offers collaborative partnerships and professional development to districts as a summer academy and an outreach program, offers coaching to teachers and leaders and provides numerous workshops on effective curriculum and leadership strategies. Dr. Cozza has transformed numerous school districts on the public and private levels to re-culture school programs to multi-age teaching and learning. In the past, she was a director of a multi-age school program and taught in an urban school system for many years. Her recent book publications include the following: co-editing a book series on school/university partnerships and authoring numerous book chapters on this topic. Her recent co-authored articles are "Principles of Effective Learning Communities in Higher Education: A Qualitative Analysis of Faculty Participation," "Effectiveness of Graduate Programs in Administration and Instructional Leadership," "Cross-Cultural Study of Cognitive and Metacognitive Processes during Math Problem Solving with Ten Year Olds,"

"Transforming Teaching: A Pilot Professional Development School Partnership," and "Interdisciplinary Studies and Connections."

Ongoing accomplishments include presenting at international and national conferences and receiving numerous grants from state and federal agencies. Dr. Cozza applies qualitative and mixed design methods in her research. She is presently senior editor for the *Journal of Applied Research in Higher Education* and a Board Member for Higher Education Teaching and Learning and is a reviewer for eight organizations and journals. Dr. Cozza mentors doctorate and master's administration students and teaches courses in the areas of curriculum, assessment, qualitative research, dissertation research seminar, and educational leadership. In the past, Dr. Cozza has been involved with accreditation processes for higher education as an NCATE SPA reviewer and a state higher education program evaluator. Dr. Cozza has a PhD degree in curriculum and instruction (language, literacy, and learning) from Fordham University and holds license certificates in School Building Leader and School District Leader.

Made in the USA
Coppell, TX
02 April 2021

52757920R00142